Lovingly,

Mother

Lovingly, Mother

The Letters of Louise Sahol Hatch
1871-1968

Compiled by
Mary Shepard Phillips & Susan Hatch Devine

Mary Shepard Phillips

AuthorHouse™
1663 Liberty Drive
Bloomington, IN 47403
www.authorhouse.com
Phone: 1-800-839-8640

© 2010 Mary Shepard Phillips & Susan Hatch Devine. All rights reserved.

No part of this book may be reproduced, stored in a retrieval system, or transmitted by any means without the written permission of the author.

First published by AuthorHouse 7/5/2010

ISBN: 978-1-4490-6680-2 (sc)

Printed in the United States of America
Bloomington, Indiana

This book is printed on acid-free paper.

Have they all come down for breakfast yet?

**The last words of Louise Sahol Hatch
according to her daughter, Edith.**

Louise Sahol Hatch in her wedding dress
1890

Introduction

Charles Hatch was born in 1895 in Battle Lake, Minnesota, a small town in western Minnesota. He became a confidant of each of his parents at a very young age. His father relied on him to help with business decisions and his mother looked to him for sympathetic understanding in her often exhausting family life. In 1914, Charles went away to Hamline University in Minneapolis and both parents continued to depend on their son for support through letters. Charles saved many of the letters from his mother, which are reproduced here along with a few that she wrote to others and several pages from her date books. Because Charles was often home over the years, especially for holidays and major family events, there are no letters marking important milestones. There is no letter concerning his father's death in 1929, for example, as of course he was at home with his mother. Other mementos, documents, letters and photographs have also been added.

Louise's letters, which date from 1914 up through 1964, tell a story of a strong, resourceful woman who raised 12 children (one a step daughter) and a niece. This is a first person history of how difficult life could be in a large family in a small town in a very cold climate in the early part of the 20th Century. Once prosperous, the family experienced financial problems during the time of most of these letters, and Louise was always concerned about money. The chores involved in cooking, baking, washing, cleaning, sewing and gardening, besides taking care of chickens and cows, required almost round the clock attention. Louise also had frequent boarders staying at the house. Keeping the house warm in winter with only small wood and coal stoves was a huge challenge.

How would Louise feel about her letters being published, with all their intimate details? Well, the fact that Charles saved them suggests that he thought they were part of our history. Now after all these years, I think she'd give us permission to use them to tell her story. It's a story set in a world completely different from ours today. On the other hand, while our world is not the same, we are still quite alike. We face many of the same dilemmas and doubts that she did. We worry about our children, have family rows, are concerned about finances and war and health and the weather. We fret about growing old. I think she'd want to tell us, "Dear ones, I did it and so can you."

I hope that the letters give tribute to the well-lived life of my grandmother, as well as serve as an appreciation of all that our own lives hold for us. In one of her last letters, Louise writes of drinking coffee on the porch, news of her children, and walking in the garden: simple essentials of her long life. "No frost yet, the garden is still nice. We enjoy corn every evening for dinner."

Mary Shepard Phillips

Table of Contents

The Hatch Family   1

The Letters of Louise Sahol Hatch   23

Coming to America   91

A. C. Hatch   101

Mementos   115

A Granddaughter's Memories   129

Notes on the Hatch Family   135

The Hatch House   151

The Hatch Family

Mama Lou and Charles
1895

Children of Adsit and Louise Hatch

A. C. Hatch   Born July 12 – 1855
Louise "   "   June 29 – 1871
Carrie Elizabeth Sept 18 – 1883
Susie Louise   Sun Dec. 28 – 1890
Agnes Camille Fri. Oct. 21 – 1892
Irene   Wed. May 30 – 1894
Charles Adsit   " Aug 14 – 1895
Hattie Olivia Thu. Oct. 21 – 1897
Edith Josephine Sat " " 1899
Clara Olive   " March 30 – 1901
Alice Olea   Sun July 13 – 1902
Irene Elizabeth Sun Oct. 23 – 1904
Dorothy Harriet Sat. July 28 – 1906
Hester Hildreth Monday Aug¹⁰ – 1908
Lorenzo Rexford Sun. Jan. 26 – 1913

The Hatch Family

Adsit Hatch   1855 – 1929
          married 1890
Louise Sahol Hatch   1871 – 1968

Children

Susan Louise   1890 – 1990

Agnes Camille   1892 – 1984

Irene   1894 – 1894

Charles Adsit   1895 – 1974

Harriet Olivia   1897 – 1976

Edith Josephine   1899 – 1991

Clara Olive   1901 – 1989

Alice Olea   1902 – 1995

Irene Elizabeth   1904 – 1999

Dorothy Harriet   1906 – 2000

Hester Hildreth   1908 – 1994

Lorenzo Rexford   1913 – 1973

Elizabeth Hatch   1884 – 1903 (Adsit's daughter)
Leila Isolde Nylander   1906 – 1934 (Louise's niece)

Louise and Libby
1889

Louise Sahol Hatch ---- Mama Lou

Louise Hansdatter was born in 1871 on a small farm near Honefoss, north of Oslo in Norway. She was baptized in 1872 and emigrated with her family in 1881 to the United States, using the surname Sahol. Louise grew up on a farm on Silver Lake in Otter Tail County, Minnesota. She attended school for the eight grades that were allowed girls then. Louise and her sisters had to help their older brothers and parents in doing chores on the farm, both in the fields and with the animals. Her mother Olea, a midwife, delivered over a thousand babies in Minnesota, including the children of the Chippewa Indians who lived on the shores of Battle Lake. Olea passed on many of her medical and herbal skills to her daughters. She also wanted them to be "ladies" and so they took lessons in the arts and crafts, such as hat making and decorative sewing. Louise excelled at oil painting.

In 1886, Louise was hired to take care of a small girl named Libby Hatch, whose mother had died. Four years later she married Libby's father, Adsit Hatch, in the parlor of his home in the town of Battle Lake. She was a beautiful bride in her black velvet wedding dress embroidered in gold. Adsit and Louise raised Libby, and had twelve children, ten daughters and two sons; Susan, Agnes, Irene (who died in infancy), Charles, Hattie, Edith, Clara, Alice, Irene Elizabeth, Dorothy, Hester and Lorenzo. A niece, Leila also grew up in the family. Louise was known by her children affectionately as Mama Lou, and for thirty years her life and days were filled with motherhood: babies and little girls and teenagers and cooking huge meals and trying to keep everyone warm. She was active in the community, especially in the Lutheran Church. She read the Bible everyday, and she was well informed about the world. One by one, the children grew up and left home. Adsit died in 1929. The family, including seventeen grandchildren came home to visit often.

Mama Lou's life was filled with dramatic events and she met her challenges with great faith and resilience. She was wise and warm and always patient. She had a deep connection to the land; in her later years, she loved to drive around to see the lakes and the fields and to walk in

9

her garden. She had a special spot in her heart for animals and birds; she adored dogs and always had one or two in the house. Her last years were peaceful and she was well cared for by her son Charles, who lived with her in the house to which she had come to in 1890. Louise died in 1968 at the age of 96. The house is still there, still standing, and remains a spirited witness to the life of Mama Lou and to all the other lives it once held. Many more generations of Hatches still love and enjoy it.

M.S.P.

Alice and Mama Lou
1902

Mama Lou and Rennie
1913

Louise with daughters, Sue and Agnes

Charles, Rennie and Mama Lou

Charles, Hattie, Mama Lou, Agnes, Edith
Alice, Leila, Dorothy, Sue, Hester, Bessie, Clara

A Family Picnic

Mama Lou, Rennie, Clara, Edith, Alice
Hester, Dorothy, Bessie

clockwise left: Leila, Bessie, Clara, Alice, Mama, Hester, Dorothy

From top: Hattie, Edith, Clara, Alice, Leila, Dorothy, Bessie, Hester

1890   1915

Mr. and Mrs. Adsit C. Hatch

Request the pleasure of your presence at the

Twenty-fifth Anniversary

of their marriage

on Tuesday evening the ninth of March

at eight o'clock

Battle Lake Minnesota

Adsit Hatch   Louise Sahol

The Hatch Family 1915

Top: Edith, Sue, Agnes, Charles, Hattie
Middle: Clara, Adsit, Louise, Alice
Bottom: Hester, Rennie, Bessie, Dorothy

Adsit and Louise

Top: Clara, Sue, Agnes, Edith, Harriet, Charles
Middle: Bess, Adsit, Louise, Alice
Bottom: Hester, Leila, Ren, Dorothy

The Letters of Louise Sahol Hatch

My dear son Charles:—

Papa is writing so I will inclose a note. Do you ever hear from Agnes? We have not heard from her since before Susie left — I can't help but worry about her — wish she would write. This is some cold weather how do you manage to live. We all went to that Church picnic — had a big feed and a short program About two hundred (200) people were there. Leila is asleep on table so must go make up beds. Lovingly Mother

The weather's so bad that people can't get to town if they want to. Been snowing hard all day and so stormy, can hardly get out at all.

Tuesday 2:30 Just finished my work and put Lorenzo to sleep which took me about one hour or more. First, I laid down with him on the bed but will never do. He rode horseback on me. He was bad to put to sleep a year ago when you used to take him and rock him to sleep but he is worse now. Do you remember when he used to tell you to sing louder. Well he is more full of tricks than he ever was. He also told us not to call him Rennie. He did not think that was big enough so I always have to say Lorenzo now.

He also told me
not to call him Rennie
He did not think that
was big enough so I
always have to say
Lorenzo now

Tuesday eve. My dear son, We have missed you so much since you left. When I came home yesterday, Rennie met me at the door and wanted to know where you were and why you did not come home. He felt pretty bad so I told him you were going to bring him a sword and a horn. Then everything was fine until bedtime. Then he thought you could come and tell him some stories. We had a long letter from Agnes which we are to forward to Sue and she is to send it to you. Uncle Ole took three old chairs up to his place to fix. That big one in my room and two little ones. Lutheran aid tomorrow. Lovingly,

Mother

I enclose $1.00, part of what I owe you.

Rennie, Charles's little brother and the youngest in the family, was about two years old. Agnes and Sue graduated from college in Minneapolis. Sue was a teacher. Agnes began nursing studies in Rochester, Minnesota. She wasn't able to come home very often and was greatly missed.

Sunday eve.

Dear Charles,

Just think you will be home in a little more than two weeks. I am so glad you went into that debate, of course you could not expect to win but it's good for you to get in with that crowd and you will know more about what is wanted when your time comes, when you ought to win.

It has been raining all day some lightning and thunder too. It sounds kind of nice like in May when I can count the days when you folks will be home. Of course I just can't think about Agnes not coming home for so long. What will we do without her?

Lorenzo thought you were coming home today. When I told him not for two weeks, he felt pretty bad.

Lovingly,
Mother

Dear Charles   To think you will be with us in a little more than a week. How glad we shall be.

This is a fine day. Everybody has gone for a walk except Edith, and she has a cold. Edith and I went to church this A.M. Shall try to get dad to go this evening.

We have not heard from Agnes for a long time but shall not worry for I know she is very busy. Mother and Uncle Ole are fine.

George Anderson's mother died of typhoid about two weeks ago and Saturday his sister Emma was buried and Mrs. Grant Marbel is in Fergus Falls hospital with it. Seems the girls took it from the mother. Hope there will be no more cases of it. The children just came home from walking and with feet as wet as rats. They go in all the water they can find.

I took off front storm windows yesterday, washed porch and windows and took paper off front door, seems a little more like summer.

Much love from,
Mother

Sunday P.M. 1-14-15

Dear Son Charles,

How is the weather down your way? So cold here keeps me busy fixing fires all the time.

Did you get that letter I sent last week with the $10.00 in it? Dad said you had no letter while he was there but I sent them to your address so I hope it was there when you got back. We have not heard from Agnes for a long time. Hope she is well.

Dad seemed to have enjoyed his visit to Minneapolis very much. Wish he could get one of those big fat paying jobs that some of them have for he seems to manage a big part of that business anyway.

I promised the girls I would make them some coffee if they would stay at home this afternoon so suppose I have to keep my work. Wish you were here too but it won't be long for the time goes so fast. It will soon be Feb. then spring. So bye, bye.

With lots of love from everybody
And God keep us all,
Mother

Adsit Hatch was a founder and first president of Hardware Mutual Insurance Company. He was now on the board of directors and went to Minneapolis for company meetings.

Wednesday eve.
Sept. 13, 1915

My dear son Charles,

We received your letter today asking for a book that you wanted Hattie to get for you at the school house. I just looked at the letter and Hattie never saw it at all. You see dad is always in such a hurry, so what did he do but take it back at noon and send it on to Agnes. He doesn't remember anything about the book so you will have to write again for it. I am very sorry about it and hope you can wait for it and I will see that it is sent that is if Hattie can get one. Rennie is here helping me write. I was going to write you last eve but papa went out to see about that machine and did not get back before between 1 and 2 o'clock so, of course, I had to go and milk old Daisie and my arm got so tired I could not write at all. Everett milked the new cow and fed the horse. He would have milked both but we did not let him know until I had milked the one. Today was Aid day at church. Took in about $5.00—pretty good. Rennie keeps bumping me so. He is on the back of my chair and keeps calling out "All aboard". His new suits came today and he put the red one right on. Today when he was going to put the cat to sleep I heard the cat had trouble and sent one of the little girls to see what the matter was. The cat got away best she could and he said, "We had a fight."
Mrs. Maden came up with a check and said they are going to move out first part of next month. He had been out of work all summer and now guess they have turned him off for good. Said he had to go where he could get work and was sorry he ever came here. Well it's too bad but it can't be helped. Hope we can rent it soon. Had letter from Agnes. She did not say to send it on so I suppose she is writing you too.

With lots of love, Mother

Everett was a handyman who helped with chores. Hattie, known as Harriet in later years, was Charlie's next in line sister. Louise was in charge of a rental property uptown that belonged to her niece, Leila. Leila came to live in the family when she was two, after her mother, Helga, Louise's sister, died of tuberculosis.

Sunday 2 P.M.

My dear boy, I will begin my Sunday afternoon work to write my children. First stop Dora came in and we talked church. Third stop. Papa came and planned his visit to Rochester next week. How I wish I could go with him. Rev. Parish was here for dinner. The children went to Sunday school and after they came home papa and I went to church.

This is such a cold day I have the little dining room table in the kitchen to write on. Lorenzo is asleep and children are playing upstairs. Baby cut his thumb Fri. not so very bad but it bled some. He was fixing an apple for himself.

Rev. Parish walked to Underwood this afternoon. He preaches there this evening. Some long walk but said he liked to so he could think better when he was alone.

Miss Clara Olson is coming Tues. to sew for us. I think her price is $1.25 a day. That is not bad. Another long stop. Papa has been talking about this trip. Say but I was sorry when I found that dad had sent your letters, clothes, book and all to the wrong address. It was too bad. Did you get your clothes in time or did you have to get others and that book came back here of course. He sent it right on again. It was too bad. What did you think? Did you think we were all dead or did you think we had forgotten our boy? I suppose you have them by this time.....hope so. We did not find out until Hattie got her card from you on Fri., no Thurs. I believe. That book you wanted Hattie to get at school house, well she has not been able to get hold of one yet but may yet—if it is not too late.

I bought some goods yesterday. Will send you samples of them. The dark blue for me. What do you think of it? The light blue for Alice and Leila. The brown for Dorothy and dark red for Bessie. Shall have to get Hester something. The silk was for my waist. I sell milk to the Swensons that live next to the hotel. They come for it so they get it for $.05. I would rather so for I can't spare children to take it. They get 2 qts most of the time and all the cream I can spare. Will send you a sample of our grapes. Papa just picked them. They are not very big but I wish we had a lot of them. We had a long letter from Agnes yesterday. Poor girl she had lost the key to her locker. Hope she will find it soon. Afraid of frost tonight. Well I must write the girls also so will have to close. Hope to hear soon if you got your clothes in time. Everybody sends love.

Lovingly Mother

Rev. Parrish was their pastor and friend. His walk to Underwood was eleven miles. Charlie sent his clothes home to be washed and ironed. There were few clothing stores in Battle Lake and buying dresses for eight girls would be very expensive so, Louise was happy to be able to hire a dressmaker.

Thurs. eve

My dear boy,
It is now 9:00 o'clock and am somewhat tired. Have been ironing since supper and made three cranberry pies for tomorrow's dinner. Am also cooking an old hen for a chicken pie for tomorrow night that I am to make for the Baptist people. They are going to give a supper. I thought I better try and help them although it seems as tho I have about all I can manage without doing for them and they gave us no small job at that.

Papa, Lorenzo and I expect to go to Fergus Falls in the morning if all is well. Want to get baby and Hester a coat. Also some little hats for the three little girls if I find any I like.

Dad is still uptown. They have a meeting about the fair. I am sorry they are going to have one. It makes so much extra work.

It is late now and not everybody in bed so must close. With lots of love from everybody.

Lovingly Mother

Battle Lake Minn.
Nov. 14, 1915

My dear son-

I will start my Sunday letters by writing you first. It is early, only 1:30. You see we only have a light dinner on Sundays now as most of us go to church.

Edith stayed at home today and got the dinner. Of course, Papa doesn't always go but he may go this evening. I hope you are in Rochester today. When I awoke this morning I could not help but feel bad when I thought how long before I could see Agnes, and she the rest of the family. I just had to make myself stop thinking that way, and only think of the good training I hope she is getting. That it may be a help to her all the rest of her life. And that the chance here at home was not anything to look forward to. I shall try to help you out a little as soon as I get a little ahead. I owed so much at the stores and have not been able to pay but very little I get. With the children all in school and cold weather coming on it takes so much. Have paid Dr. Hectnor a little but we owed him about $24 and a lot more work will have to be done for Edith and Clara. Papa ought to go too. It has been very cold the last three days. It is hard work to keep the house warm. Hope I get the stove up in my room this week. You may help put up coal stove when you get home.

If ever you come across a sugar bowl I would like one for everyday use, as the children broke my white one and I hate to use my best one. I also want a pair of leggings for Lorenzo in red knit with draw string at waist - can't get them big enough here, of course. I can send if you don't just happen to see any. I don't know just what they will be worth about $.75 or $1.00 not more.

Lovingly, Mother

Dr. Hectnor was the dentist.

Edith, Clara and Alice were considered the middle children and Bessie, Dorothy, Leila and Hester were the "little girls" and baby Rennie came along in 1913.

Thursday 2:30 P.M. (1915)

My dear boy, Received your letter this A.M. Rennie is so happy about the card he got. It is warming up a little. We washed Mon. eve. We started the machine at 5:00 o'clock and we finished in about 2 hours. It rained all that night and the next day so our clothes only got dry yesterday. Will iron your shirt and try to get it off on the train if I can. Think Hester can take it up for me. Bessie's shoes from Sears Roebuck came today. They are a strong well made shoe. Shall get more the same kind for the others.

Yes, my boy your name is written higher than the capitol dome can ever reach and it's only for you to see that it remains there. I am not worrying. I know our boy will make good.

I do so hope Agnes can come home Christmas.

Well I better get this off. It is too late.

Lovingly, Mother

Washing clothes took hours; heating water, using a scrub board and a hand wringer. During the winter the clothes still had to dry outside and would often freeze. The sheets and shirts and all were like boards and were stacked up on the porch at night until they could thaw and hopefully dry when the sun came out.

Battle Lake, Minn. Dec., 1915

Dear Charles, Almost a week since you left. This has been a busy one about the house. Washed all the storm windows and the others on the outside too and got them all on. One big job done. Had the Lutheran Aid in the new basement, that also made a lot of extra work. Cleaned the store room and Hester, Bessie and Dorothy filled it full of wood. We also got some more meat, I had to take care of too. Shall make our mincemeat, first part of week. The play given for or by the social center did not take as well as the one you people gave last winter, and I guess they did not do so very well. They go to Maine Monday evening and Underwood Tuesday night. A little hard on Dorothy I am afraid but she says they are all so good to her. Edith also is in it. Shall be so glad when they are done, for it breaks in on our time so. I made Mr. and Mrs. Hopkins come in and look at our piano. They did not seem to want to but I talked and then talked some more. They seemed to want Bill Olson to get them one. They said he could get a good one for $240 so I hope they will not get that much and we will have a chance.

Have to go get children to bed before church time. Will finish when we get back. Rev. McCracken is to be at the church tonight.

Monday A.M. It got so late last night before we got home. We heard a fine sermon and the church was so full some had to go away. It is so dark I believe it's going to snow. One day Dora asked Rennie for a kiss and he said, "No, one day I kissed a lot of girls and it made me so sick." He is telling now what he is going to give everybody for Christmas. Guess we are all going to get horns.

Lovingly, Mother

Louise wanted to sell the piano to the Hopkins who lived next door because she needed the money. The piano is still in the Hatch house and still plays. It's arrival in 1906 was noted in the newspaper and most of the children took piano lessons. Agnes Camille was the most serious student. Dorothy played the wedding march on it for Clara's marriage in the parlor.

Wednesday night

My Dear Son, Have just a few minutes before children's bedtime so
will start a letter. I have been up until after 12:00 for two nights to wait
for Dorothy. They played at Underwood Mon. night and Maine Tues. I
am so glad they are done with that only to begin to fix for another Fri.
eve given by the school. Leila, Dorothy, Hester, Alice and I don't know
how many more are in that.

Edith is not well. Came home sick yesterday noon and has been in bed
ever since with a cold and seems to be all tired out. Bessie came home
this afternoon and went to bed. She is not bad and expects she will
be all right in the morning. Leila too felt a little off and did not go to
school this afternoon. Hattie got a bad bump in basketball game last
night. Had to go to Hectnor to get her front teeth straightened. She
looks bad--let me see is that all our trouble. Oh! No the worst is yet to
come so prepare yourself. Toots (the cat) is on the chase; has to live in
the back room but he comes right in the minute the door is open. Guess
he is ours to keep. Shall send Agnes a box tomorrow if possible. Am sort
of tired so much going on among the children. Well, it's bedtime for the
children. Well I thought I had put the little folks to bed so I could write
some more when out comes that brother of yours and tells me I am not
good to him if I don't let him stay up, and it's 10:00 and after. Rennie
says Mike is trying to sing. He is outside growling something awful.

John has fixed up the window at the store very nice. Has that big red
hanging lamp lit evenings and the new goods are all here. Must take
baby to bed so good night.

Thursday eve. Dear Charles, This letter did not go off today so will add
a line. Andrew Stoa was here today. Came down to see his father. Edith
came downstairs for a little while today but is not very well. Papa also is
on the bum and most of the children feel a wee bit out of sorts. Guess
it is the weather.

Must go up and take care of Edith and then to bed so good night again
and love from all, Mother.

*The children were in a play that was performed in neighboring towns.
Andrew Stoa was Louise's cousin. John worked at the hardware store.*

Sunday afternoon
Dec. 15, 1915

My Dear Son Charles, Have just finished letter to Agnes. To think Sue will be with us in one week and less time before you will be home. Edith has been sick in bed most all week but is up and better now. Lots of colds around the children. I believe one snow would make things better althou this is fine weather for Dec. Dad is uptown. Children want something to eat so will have to stop for a little while.

Called on Mother and had supper and time for church. Miss Rumsey sent me some Christmas lily bulbs also. Hattie, Edith, and Clara all go up to Fergus Falls to basketball game Fri. I will send underwear tomorrow. Sorry I have been so slow but sent Agnes a box yesterday and had some sewing to get done for her.

Lovingly, Mother

Battle Lake Minn.
Jan. 8, 1916

My dear son Charles,

It seems like an age since you left. Tomorrow you will see dad; wish I could go down with him but, of course, that cannot be. Yesterday when Lorenzo got up he felt so bad and said I wish Charles would not stay so many days. I suppose Susie has seen Agnes by this time.

Papa and I went to Lutheran Church Saturday evening.

After dinner I took some dinner up to Mother and Uncle Ole. They are both sick. Yesterday I washed your stuff also took home some washing from the Svenson Family. Mrs. Albert Larson took some and Mrs. Christie took a little. They seem to have a hard time. The mother is in bed and so many little children.

Will send your underwear tomorrow.

I am feeling much better than when you left and I am so glad because then I can work and keep busy and get out some for I miss you children so much. Just have to fight that awful feeling that gets me when Lorenzo and I are alone. So we try to look forward to your homecoming and play we are busy getting ready for you. Did you hear a good sermon this day?

Papa wants some coffee so will close and I have several more to write to.

With much love from your Mother

Louise's mother, Olea Sahol lived in the apartment uptown with her brother, Ole Stoa. Louise's father, Hans, died in 1909.

Battle Lake, Minn.
Jan. 13, 1916

My dear Son Charles,

Clara and some of her friends are cooking candy in the kitchen.

This has been a pretty hard week. Shall be glad when dad gets here. Hope he is well so he can get to work. This has been the coldest weather. The little ones have been at home for two days and the big ones took their dinners. Yesterday "Wed" it was 38 below with a high wind at night. It went down to 40 or more. I thought we would freeze to death. Sat up until eleven to keep fires and then up and down all night and for all the wood it takes it has kept me busy every minute. Wood, water, chickens, children and all the other work and then I took a terrible fall on some ice in the kitchen two days ago and all but killed myself. My right arm and back is very much on the bum. John has been so good. Helped bring in wood and this morning he made a path to the chicken house for me. I was so surprised when I came out and found a good road. Yesterday I went down full length if I had been longer I'd gone deeper, but of course it blew so all day it would have done no good to make roads then. Tonight I shall bring the kitchen into my room. Last night everything froze so hard thought I never could get a thing fit to eat. The bread was as hard as stones. Got Rennie's slippers today. Rennie sits in papa's place at the table and we have to call him papa all the time. He sits in Papa's big chair by the coal stove and holds his pipe in his hand. Well, shall have to start to move in from kitchen and get in wood for the night. This looks bad but it is the only paper I could find so please excuse. The girls are fooling so I can't write. With lots of love from everybody, Mother

Wednesday Eve.

Dear Sue and Charles--

Sent a box today but did not have time to write then. Got Sue's letter this P.M. Am truly sorry that you have so much trouble but we all have ours. I thought I had mine today when all the High School children came home at noon and were mad as could be about their marks. No one got what they thought they ought to have. That Miss Wollie or Wahler or something you know. Well, they all hate her more than the rest if that is possible but don't seem to like anyone a little bit—school or work. And I do get so tired of it all. I can't help but feel a little hard toward the teachers myself for I don't think they amount to a thing They do get big pay and have a good time. Most of them do. Last evening I had to help Dorothy find some things. It took up all my evening so I could not get my letters written. Wish Miss Jones would do her own work and not send them home for their Mothers to do. I for once have had enough. If I should write all I feel tonight about teachers and their work I am afraid it would not look very well. I think I would like to use a D (word). Now I know that is not a bit nice.

Clara's coat is not very good. We may not keep it. Bessie's hat is nice. Yesterday Gordon Bondy and Lorenzo went to the lake and took off their shoes and socks and went in wading. Do you hear from Agnes?

Mother

Thursday, A.M.

I just want to say Bessie had not been sick in bed and we have had no Dr. She is just poorly but is up everyday and helps about the house. Was afraid you would think her bad.

Dodo went to school this A.M. Snow will cover her up to her ears but not so very cold so she will make it O.K. Took her dinner. The other little ones are at home. Bye, bye.

With love from,
Mother

Dodo was a nickname for Dorothy.

Sept. 17, 1916

My dear son Charles,

I am so sorry we could not find that book you wanted. I first sent the girls to look but when they said they could not find it I went over every room after they had looked but all in vain.

A week ago now we were all walking in the garden and picking plums by the brick house. Then we all had coffee together. Today Dad and I will have our coffee alone. I am writing at the kitchen table—the house is so cold, and the little girls are playing in the dining room.

Think Dad is uptown. Many of us went to church this morning and the rest will go tonight. How did you spend your Sunday?

Would like to take one peep at Sue just now and see what she is doing. I can't help but think she would have liked the schoolroom better. We shall be so glad to see Sue when she gets back and talk over things with her for she left in such a hurry.

We washed Friday after school and it started to rain that evening and rained ever since except a little while last evening so we got most of the clothes in but too late to iron as we had planned to do. It is clearing up now but froze some of the garden stuff just a little, not much harm was done.

We hope to get the little stove set up tomorrow. We have a roomer here. A boy that Mrs. West asked me to take. He may stay 3-4 weeks and I get $1.25 per week. He is no trouble. Comes late and goes early. The girls have not seen him yet as they are not up in the morning when he goes off. They are so anxious to see what he looks like. I tell them he is very handsome—never saw one quite so good looking before. I rather think that will bring them up a little earlier in the morning. The man's name is Matt or Mark Johnson. Well, the boys just came home and Dad wants his coffee so must close. With lots of love from us all and hopes and good wishes for my son and may you be able to gather much good and profit well by this year's investment.

Mother

Tues. eve

Dear Charles, Just about to go to bed. So tired. Been trying to sew some today. Hester is wearing her best dress to school. The only one she has. As to your going to see Agnes I can't say as I can help out on it. Just now there is so little I have coming in and so much going out this year. Wish I could help you out on it—if it had only been a little later or if I had known I might have saved a little. So you will have to do as you think best. As for Agnes I am not worrying at all. Had letter from her this P.M. She seems to feel fine again. Will enclose her letter if I find it. Now I will talk about the family. Edith came home from school sick. She went right to bed and vomited about every five minutes. Alice went over to take care of Carl William so his mama could go up town then she was taken sick over there and kept Edith T. busy cleaning up after her. Of course, she came home as soon as she could.

At supper time Bessie began chasing for the bucket and just a little while ago Hester joined the rest. Had to laugh. It is something like that sweet summer night if you remember only not so bad.

Papa had his turn last Sat. and Rennie Sunday night. They are all over their trouble by now and hope the rest will get over theirs as quick. Hattie and Clara were laughing at the way the others were kept busy but I told them to remember that the one who laughs last, laughs best. Well, I guess the rest is all right now. I think that is all about the family. Don't you wish you were here to join the crowd? I don't feel like flying very high myself tonight but that is an old story so that is all right.

This is as far as I got last night and will just add a word to let you know how we are. At 11:00 last night Leila was taken. At 2:00 I began, then the cat and dog and I had to clean up after them. Hattie also had a bad night. The poor rug got it bad. I have been cleaning and washing up stuff all morning. Have the upstairs left. Hattie, Edith and Alice all went to school. Don't know how long many of them will stay. The rest all got out and dressed so we will soon be O.K. Clara is at home tonight. She is the only one real well. I must close as she is going uptown to mail this.

Love from Mama

Wednesday Eve Nov. 1, 1916

My dear Son Charles, Alice is writing so will enclose a line from her. I have just written Sue also so our Sunday letters were short. As to your going on the road next summer, well how do you suppose we could do without you, business and all and Dad seemed very much hurt and said it would not be much of a summer without you.

You know Dad needs you and we must hope that next year will be better than this one has been, although Dad has done fine in wheat and potatoes this fall but the other part of the business is very slow. Dad works hard to save on extra help. He and the little ones are in bed now and Alice and I are writing; the rest are out. This is a beautiful night. Hope tomorrow will be nice for we are going to clean up the yard. Well, I got off my subject. May God bless the book agents and I am sorry for them but I believe this year will be a slow one for even them as money is tight somehow.

There was an oldish lady here yesterday. She had a set, I think something in the order of the classic books to sell. Of course, I told her I could not think of it. She was very nice about it but I could see when she came that she thought she had me. I was sorry for her for I knew she could not do much in B.L. for we have had too many of late and people don't buy what they can do without. Dad said the other day he had talked with J. B. Thompson about a car for next summer. He seems to think we ought to have one. You never said anything about the box with the duck. Now did you like it or don't you eat ducks? I could not remember but thought you could give it to someone that did. I was sorry there was not anything left of the fair stuff to send you a sample but Bessie sold her cake to Mrs. Grant for $0.50 and the other went for Sunday. How did that pie come through or was it all mush? How much time do you get Thanksgiving?

Good night and may God keep my boy, Lovingly Mother

Charles thought of spending the summer selling books on the road but he was needed at the store. Many door to door salespeople came through town.

Sunday Eve. Nov. 5, 1916

Dear son—Well this has been another busy Sunday. Rev. Parish preached this A.M. and we all went. They took dinner with Rev. Ackley's folks. Mrs. Parish and the children were here also and they took supper with us and, of course, I did not know that they would be here until about 4:30 so had to plan things quick as they had to start for Underwood at 6:30. Mr. Waldo took them. Mr. Parish preaches there tonight. Stoas drove up. They did not stay only a short time. They brought his father some things and us a cat. I told her last Sun., when they were here, that we had to get one as the mice are getting so bad in the kitchen. But since they had two, they said we could have the one so they brought it, while the roads are good. I made some coffee for them. Stoa's father is not very well. He hurt his foot.

This week we have Sunday School convention here. I'm expecting to entertain some and we will have aid here. Hope we have a big crowd.

We had no school Thurs. and Fri., Teacher's convention. So we did some house cleaning. Cleaned my room so it is ready for the stove to go in. Also we had the rug out and the parlor one too and cleaned a lot outside so things look pretty good now.

The children got a little better marks in school this week although some did not do as well as they ought to. The wind is blowing hard tonight. Guess we will have a change in the weather. Last week was fine. Children home from League and it's time for church so must close. Mr. Parish said you were looking fine and doing well also.

Lovingly, your
Mother

Stoas are Louise's relatives on her mother's side.

Monday evening. Everybody gone to bed but as I did not get your letter off today will just add a note. I am so glad you are coming home soon. When you come be prepared to wade in. Dad and I had a little misunderstanding again tonight. Sorry I said what I did to him but I just can't help it sometimes or I would go all to pieces. Tonight it was about John L. I know he is not much good but I cannot help that part of it and I guess they are not doing much of any thing nor have they all fall. John went out Sat. and they said he had sold a spreader but I found today nothing was done. Then there was some deal in Ottertail that Bing got ahead of them. Well tonight Papa said he was going to tell J.L. a lot of things in the morning. You see I guess I stirred it up a little to begin with but I get so tired of them saying what they do whey they don't do a thing and I told Papa so and that he was to blame that he could not get mad when things were not done but see that it was done and this is what hurt the worst and I ought not have brought your name into it but I did. I said you said last summer that they were all too slow and did not look after things as they should. Of course, Papa felt very hurt but I can't help it. If I looked after my part of the business in a way he does we would not have bread to eat nor clothes to wear. I know and I don't know if it is a sin to stir up a little dirt of this kind. Sometimes it almost seems as if it had to come. I told him he had no right to always get mad at his help if they were no good. Just let them down easy and not act like a mad man but to keep awake himself and I think the rest will go well. I may not send this. Will see how I feel in morning may be better. So if you don't get a letter from dad for a day or two you will know but he knows it's the truth. That is why it hurts I suppose.

It has snowed all day. Very cold. John L. and Papa put up bedroom stove today. Shall be glad when coal stove is up. It is hard to keep house warm with that little one.

10:30 now so must get to bed so I can get out in morning on time.

Lovingly, Mother

Sunday Eve.

Dear Charles, This cold weather coming on so fast has made it rather busy, about this place. Sat. P.M., Bess, Hester and I worked out in garden and raked leaves for bedding for pigs and cow. Shoved the boat up by the rabbit pen. I did not know till just now what made my arms so sore. The feed is getting low but Dad has ordered some corn and the pig will last just as long as the corn lasts. I have been trying hard to think of a man to help at store while dad goes to convention next week. It will be hard living around her if he can't.

I must put Ren to bed. He is asleep now in dad's big chair. Will finish later.

Monday   Dad says trade good Sat. and today. Sold three or four stoves.

Sunday eve 11/12/16

My dear son—Just back from church. It's very cold out and in too for we have only the little stove in the front room and we all hug up to that. Edith is going to stay home tomorrow to help wash storm windows and clean up a little. We are to have the aid Wed.

Leila has been out of school a few days because of a cold. She is better and may go back tomorrow. Did I or anyone write about Hattie stepping on a nail. She was bad for several nights and days. Called the Dr. 11:30 the first night. He fixed it up and she is going back to school tomorrow if I can get anyone to take her. Of course, she can't get her shoe on for sometime.

We have not heard from you all week except one letter first of the week have we? And no letter from Agnes at all. Dad wants something to eat so will finish later.

47

Nov. 19, 1916

Dear Son Charles, I have a few minutes before church time. Shall go
to the Lutheran Church tonight as there is no preaching in any of the
other churches and they have English services there.
We got our new bookcase Sat. and we had enough books to fill it.

We put up a stove in our room this week but there is a lot to do yet
so hope it will keep nice weather a little longer.
Hattie is about well. She walked to school Fri.

Must put Lorenzo to bed before I go today. I told him you would
soon be home and I wish you could have seen him. He was so happy.
May Good keep us all another week.

Lovingly, Mother

Sunday eve. 11-26-16

Dear Son Charles,

Had planned to write sooner but time will not permit. No church for us today.

This will be a lonely Thanksgiving Day with you all gone but then we have a lot to be thankful for and must remember that. I am sorry the outlook for Agnes coming home for Christmas is small. She could only stay a day or two and then it will cost a lot although I would love to see her so much for when she was here we were so busy and the house full of folks so we did not have as good a time as we ought to have had.

I failed to see the sport in the burning of peoples' houses and sheds for, of course, they belong to poor people (our style) for the rich would not have moveable houses of that sort. I know how I should feel if anyone carried off some of our truck for it would be hard to replace even the wood box this year. Butter is 40 cents and lard 23 cents. Don't know what eggs are worth as I had some packed. Four weeks from this evening will be Christmas Eve.

This has been a fine day. Had the doors open all morning. Seemed sort of like spring only the days are so short.

Business is so poor I don't understand this as everything is so high that is the farmers get such good prices for everything they have that they ought to be able to pay up and do something.

I bought cream and made butter this week. Cream at 20 cents a quart is not bad. Can make our butter for about 26-27 cents per pound. A little extra work but it is worth the while. May as well close as I can't think of anything to write. Children are tired and the folks talk so good night and love from,

Mother

12-3-16

Dear son Charles—Just finished a letter to Agnes. Poor dear, it will seem so hard not to have her with us at Christmas time—not to expect her or look forward to her homecoming with the rest of you. We shall miss her so. Hope she will not feel so very bad about it.

Our boys came back today but as it is Sunday and they know I don't like to do business on that day they have not paid. May do so in the morning and if they do shall send it on to you for I know you must need some by this time.

This has been a beautiful day. Hope we may have many more as it will help shorten the winter.

Our Thanksgiving was a lonely one. We missed you all so but then we ought to give thanks just the same for the many blessings we receive every day.

Dad surely is true to you. He writes you about every day but I often wonder if he ever writes the girls anymore. Whenever I ask him he says, well I must write Charles first.

We went to church this morning but Dad did not want to go this evening so I shall stay home too.

Shall try to get your laundry sent soon.

Lovingly, Mother

"Our boys" are farm children who pay to stay at the Hatch house during the school week.

Wednesday evening

Dearest big brother,

Mama is darning some stockings and will add to this later on, but I am to start this for her. Hattie has been sick and is in bed now. She has a cold. Edith is not feeling very well either. She has been out of school all day. Mama is going to send two of your shirts tomorrow, so that you will get them for Sunday. Your washing came just as we were all through with our washing, so mama got Mrs. Swanson to wash them. She will send the other soon.

So good night, Lovingly, Clara

Dear Son Charles- I did not have time to add to this before. Been very busy. Miss Nelson told me this morning that she could come for a little while so, of course, I got ready for her. She worked on Hattie's dress until 4:00 o'clock. I shall do the rest myself with Hattie's help. Hattie got up today. Will try to go back to school tomorrow. This P.M. I went to Mrs. Christie's aid for a little while.

Had letter from Agnes today. She did not know if she could get away and I don't know what to do if she does for I can't help out with money as I had expected to do and Dad is worried so about business most of the time so I feel we must be as careful as possible. Shall write her tonight or in morning. Lots of love, from Mother

Miss Nelson was a dressmaker.

Sunday eve

Dear Charles—Papa has written so will just enclose a note with his. Children are looking for that box and about their overshoes, I think I will wait and send for them so I get them here by the time school opens after Christmas. That will be soon enough. Am reading "Inside the Cup" quite a book. Shall give it away but don't know who to yet. We will have our Christmas when you and Sue get here. I do not see how Sue can get here Christmas Eve do you?

Children and dad all have been off for a week or more.

I did want some hair ribbons for the girls but as I can't send money this time and you may not go downtown before you leave, we will let it go.

Lovingly, Mother

Sunday Eve. Dec. 10, 1916

Dear Charles, Have just finished a letter to Agnes. Someways I feel so bad about Agnes not coming home this year but, of course, it can't be helped. I hope she won't mind it much.

Got your laundry too late but shall have Mrs. Severson wash two of the shirts. Hope that will help you out until I wash again.

We all went to church this morning except Alice. If you want anymore money tell Dad as I may not get any money until too late for you.

Too dark to see much more so shall start supper and look after chickens. I never get an egg anymore. It is going to be colder tonight. Have a little snow. Looks like a heavy frost.

Lovingly, Mother

Sunday eve 1-10-17

My dear son Charles:

I wrote you a letter last Sunday but we never sent it because we were all snowed in so long I lost it. Hope you got Dad's letter and the $15.00 I gave him to send. Sorry it was not more

Edith and Clara left for Pelican Rapids and as the train did not wait they got off and had to stay in Fergus until Saturday and had their game Saturday evening and will come back here Monday. We heard they lost both games although it was close.

I went to church this morning.

You must put in full time and then some if you take 21 hours of work. Is that what you are going to do? Miss Walher (guess that is not spelled right) took 15 hours and thought she had all she could do. Well, Charles I am glad you do your best and your Mother is proud of her boy and very thankful that you are able to do so well.

This week – Wednesday, I think, we had a dreadful scare about Agnes when a letter I had sent her about two weeks ago came back unclaimed because Ed Rudle also came back from Rochester unable to see her although he had called two times while there. So we telegraphed Harold S. and asked him to go and be sure to see her but, of course, we could not get an answer until next morning so, of course, we did not sleep much that night. I could only think of all the things they might have done for we had not heard from her for over two weeks and then she asked why we did not write so she must have missed getting more letters. Well, we felt better when Harold sent word he had seen her and that she was all right and then the next day brought a long letter from her.

Lorenzo said it must be a pony you are going to send him as long as it has legs or walks. He said you did not write your letters right. You forgot to close them—that is you did not say you were going to close, so he did not think it finished. He loves to carry your letters around with him as long as there is a thing left of them and I have to read them over and over to him. He says Dad's initials are P.A. because papa spells P.A.

Did Rack go to war?

53

What do you think about this dreadful war question? I pray we may be spared and that the Lord will not forsake us.

Basketball was very popular and many of the Hatch children played on school teams.
They went to games at neighboring towns on the train.
Louise was very concerned about World War I.
Rack was C.J. Wittbecker, daughter Sue's husband, who was in the Army.

I was up at mother's this afternoon and also evening. She is not well and I had to fix her up some.

Poor dad has been out of sorts most all week. I do not know if it is war or business or what. I do hope things will brighten up some. I can only turn to the one that has promised to help and stand by us, but of course Dad has not found this friend that is ever ready to help if we only ask. He only tries to struggle along alone and finds it rather hard to find his own way alone and in the dark as it were.

A week ago Fri. we had Mallery's over for supper. They were here til almost twelve and seemed to enjoy the visit. I shall be so glad when this cold weather lets up a little for it does make work so hard.

Hope we hear from all of you soon. With love from Mother

P.S. Our folks got back from Pelican Rapids this A.M. Lost both games but had a good time while there and it did not cost them anything.

We received your letter this A.M. but not Lorenzo's present. We are going up now so may get it. More love Mother

Sunday 1-28-17

My dear son Charles:

Just finished a letter to Agnes. Poor girl seems to be so homesick. Thanks for stockings I received. They are lovely but you should not have bought them or such good ones anyway.

This is the first nice day we have had for a long time and it seems so good. It makes me think of spring and the time you will all be here again. Makes me sort of homesick for you all.

The children's colds are better although they cough a little yet. Rennie is up now and thinks he will go back to school tomorrow. We washed yesterday and today the clothes are drying good on the back porch so will try to get yours off early in the week.

Dad seems to have done well with the last grain he sold. At the end of this week four weeks of school will be finished so I will get my pay from the boys. I hope for sure the first of next and will send it right off as soon as I get it for you all.

I can smell the coffee. I put it on when I started this so guess it is ready. Wish you were here to have some with us in the kitchen.

Shall be glad when chickens begin business so I can bake more and send off a few boxes. Our cow is doing fine but too late to sell any milk as everybody got fresh cows at same time we did, but the calf will be worth something after awhile. Well it's coffee time so bye, bye. With lots of love from Mother

Sunday eve 2-4-17

Dear son Charles,

Read your letter and we are proud of our boy and the good marks you are getting and that you are making good use of your time while there.

This has been a dreadful day so cold and stormy. It is the worst day we have had for a long time. It makes lots of hard work. Also shall be so glad when we get a change. Everything in the house froze up last night even in the dining room, with big fire in the stove too.

Wonder how Sue stands it. She has been sick too with a cold. The boys did not go home this week so expect I shall have to wait until their folks can send up some money for them before I get mine. The boys have not been home since Christmas.

Fri. evening we had Mrs. and Mr. Mallery over for supper. They did not go home until almost twelve o'clock. Mrs. M. played games with the children and seemed to have a good time. We had ice cream too as our new cow is doing very well.

It is so cold in dining room. Shall have to close and go and hug the stove. What do you know of Rack and what do you think about war for this country? Let's pray that we may be spared.

The children's colds are much better but there will be no school for them tomorrow if it is this bad. We washed Sat. and the clothes are out on back porch full of snow. Had to pick some up that had blown down this morning. Much love from us all and may God keep us safe.   Mother

Sunday 2-18-17

Dear son Charles--

It will only be a short letter today as I have many I ought to write and the day is far gone. Went to church this AM and up to Mothers this PM and fixed her all up. She is a little better but getting along very slowly.

I sent you part of your laundry, will send rest soon as I can get it done. Shall send Agnes a box tomorrow. I gave dad $10 and he said he made it $15. Hope you got that O.K. Next letter if you do not need quite that much you let me know what you want as I can use the extra very well as there are so many things the girls want but I don't want you to go hungry or skrimp.

We got two eggs yesterday. Our boys went home over Sunday—Just got back so will have to get supper for them.

Lovingly,
Mother

Sunday eve 2-25-17

Dear Charles—I had planned to go to church this evening but don't like to go alone so guess I will stay at home and write letters. Dad and the children are playing rummy. Not quite so cold tonight but lots of snow. Hope there will soon be a change in this weather. Easter Sunday, April 8th, what time do you get off then and are you arriving home? Sue seemed to think she can't. Mother is feeling much better and so is Uncle Ole.

There seems to be nothing I can write about this evening. I guess I am not in the mood for writing so will close as Alice and Clara will be able to write something of interest. Love from Mother.

Sunday P.M. 3-4-17

Dear son Charles-

Just finished dinner and girls are just finishing up the work now. Hattie, Edith, Alice and I went to church this morning. It's so cold as ever-16 below this morning and it makes everybody tired and out of sorts. This has been one long hard winter and I shall be glad when we get a break so we can plan things and talk things over. There is a lot to be done this spring and summer.

Dad and I are invited to Mallery's for supper tomorrow evening. Lorenzo too but the walking is so bad guess he will not go. We washed Sat. and shall send your laundry soon as I can get it dry. We killed our calf this week so we have some nice meat but our chickens won't do a thing. Our poor cat got sick and died Fri.

Much love and may God keep us all. Mother

Thursday 7 am

Dear Charles—Got your letter yesterday. Edith went to work a little before 6 this morning and also worked from 11-7 yesterday. I do miss her help at home. Don't think there will be much dusting done.

My money is due Fri. so I will send you it as soon as I get my hands on it so you would not have to ask dad for any before you come.

I wish the chicken pen was fixed. I have to spend ½ of my time chasing chickens off the neighbors' doorsteps. You see dad took the east side of the fence down to move it up so as to make the garden bigger on the east side but he never has time to fix anything. Well the folks are down for breakfast so I must close.

Lovingly,
Mother

Monday eve 4/9/17

My dear son—I am holding Lorenzo at the dining room table while I write you a note. He feels so bad because you went. He is trying to count the weeks until you come back. He was brave until we got uptown on our way home from the station but when we got as far as the drug store he broke down and wept all the way home.

Our people are here that is they were here when I came home. We are all in the front room now. Sort of cold and the fire feels good. Dad and Mr. Bullock are talking war. Mrs. B. is reading and I shall fix your stockings now so I can get them off in the morning. This seems strange—not just like home but oh I am so glad and hope they stay.

It is hard to get used to you in St. Paul again but better there than as if you had gone to war so I can only say "all is well" and may God keep us all.

With love,
Mother

Tues. A.M. Boys came and also Mrs. McCalla, the corset lady. Got to fix Sue's room for her now.

Mr. and Mrs. Bullock were boarders at the house for a time.

60

Sunday P.M. 4/22/17

My dear son-

Mr. Parish just left. He preached this morning. Took dinner at Ackley's then made a short call here. I asked him to because I wanted to talk over the Ausbury Hospital plans for Hattie with him. He was very much pleased and said he would write them so I think everything will be all right although he said the Wright's Hospital in Fergus was fine and not so hard and if Hattie found Ausbury too hard she could change to Wrights. Mr. Parish also said he had taken Sue's case up with Supt. Norby at Fergus Falls so if there is a chance she will get it. I thought that very kind of him.

Our chicks came off Fri. and Sat.—poor luck only got 14 and one of them died last night so have only 13 left but their eggs were no good.

I bought a sack of sugar with the Bullock money ($9.00) and am glad I could for it has gone up since I got it.

We had little Carl here Saturday. His mother was in Fergus Falls. Mrs. Teller said Saturday was a big day in Fergus Falls. About 60 men went to war.

I am thinking of our boy night and day for we just could not spare him and we don't want to. I pray the war may end before it begins. It is all in God's hands so let us all pray that we may have peace.

Did you get that check I sent a few days after you left? Mr. S.A. Swanson got a new car. They took Dad and I out for a ride. Had a fine time although it was a little cold.

Lorenzo doesn't feel very well has a little cold and it makes him so cross. Hope we hear from you soon.

Lovingly,
Mother

Monday eve.

Dear Charles, This is my first letter to you since you left but shall try to do better after this. There is always so much to be done and when the work is done I don't feel like writing. Edith has not been very well since Christmas but seems to feel better now. That has made it rather hard and these everlasting chores but it is all getting better. Dad milks and pumps a lot of the water, of course, we bring it in. Have only one calf to feed now. The other one made a little over 75 pounds of dressed meat. Very nice. I had a little trouble with John Rostad about the hay he sent us. It was slough hay and wire grass and the cow would not eat it so I called him up and asked him if he thought he had done the right thing and if his conscience would let him rest and my cow was going dry so he sent a man to take it away. I have not been able to get anymore yet and have only enough good hay to last a few days. The roads are very bad and no one likes to go. Waiting for more snow so sleighing will be better.

The folks all went to the movies this eve but I had to cut up a pig I got from Erickson today and as I wash tomorrow I had to get the thing out of the way. Cost me 13 cents per pound which is not so bad. Dad is so restless and upset—wants to start something. He has been on edge for several days.

It doesn't bother me as it used to. I just say yes to everything and laugh when he gets so foolish and hikes off. No business at all very dull all over.

Well the movie folks are here so can't write much more as it is late and we must get to bed. Had letter from Hattie. She asks everybody to write. We entertained the teachers Sat. eve. and a few more, guess Dodo told you all about it.

I will send your money soon.

Shall try to get your laundry done first of this week.

Lovingly,

Mother

Harriet left to enroll in the nursing program at Ausbury Hospital.

62

Sunday am

Dear Son, You have got to come home. John Drew signed up for the Navy so that leaves me all alone. Geo Willie will help a day or two. All the boys are on the list. They are as follows:

Wm. Gustafson, C. Hiller, B.F. Ackley and Frank Stuckman (officer's squad). Melvin Hackson, Carlton Byrr, Melvin Severson, Rudolf Olson. Lew Larson, Geo. Stiner, Wm. Olson, Carl Ranstad, Archie Anderson. Battle Lake's full quota. Swift and young Rodney may sign up and several from the town will go the whole tour. All the people of the county about will be at the train to see them off. Now Chas I am mighty glad you did not go in, but I hear said that they stated to you that you were rather late, and your eyes would disbar you in any event and that you could not be considered until they were in better shape.

    Well I will mail this in the morning. May add some.

Good night,
Dad

A.C. Hatch was in charge of filling Battle Lake's quota of men for the draft in World War I.

May 2nd, 1917

Dear Son, Perhaps I did not explain matters yesterday. Well, they want 2500 men for officers commissioned. They go into a training camp and get prepared to take charge of the army drafted later. Now you stand as good a show as anyone. I think it will do no harm if you fail and it won't take but a little of your time as the age limit will probably be 21-27. It will bring about all of that age in the 2 million call. You will get a better show as an officer 1st or 2nd Lieut. than a private. You can do as you think. Yesterday was a cold drizzly day. Took in about $25 cash about $10 on the books. Today is bright but cool. Froze this A.M. Am setting out new bed of strawberries. Ren is not strong yet but his appetite is fairly good now. Think he will be all OK when the weather gets settled.

As ever, Dad

Dear son Charles—This is all I can find to write on. Did not get my Sun. letter off so will add a little more before I send it. I do not know what your father has written you in regard to the war but I do hope your eye trouble will keep you from enlistment. They seem to be very careful of whom they take and your eyes are very bad at times that is sure. We can't spare you anymore than if you were the head of this household for we need you right now. Dad is more interested in war and the country's welfare right now than in his own business although he doesn't know it.

Had long letter from Agnes. She is well. The sun shined today although not in my heart. May God help to keep us all and our country in peace. Mother.

These letters concern Charlie's possible service in the army during W.W. I. Adsit suggests that he enlist and become an officer and Louise advises him that his poor eyesight should make him ineligible. Charlie did not join and before he was called the war was over.

Thursday eve 10:30

Dear Charles, I suppose you will think my letters come thick and fast but I can't help it. I have no one else to tell my troubles to except God and he knows I have enough. I don't know what to do with your father. He seems so worked up over something, I sometimes wonder if he is not just a little off. He just raves over any little thing and it is so hard with the boys and Bullocks in the house and the poor children that must know all this. This evening Mrs. Severson got her ears full. Her door was open and she was coming out just when dad had a spell on the back porch. She shut the door and went in but I am sure she will be busy tomorrow and for sometime to come to tell all she knows and I don't blame her. I sometimes wonder if a drunk man is worse than a crazy one. I think a drunk one is better of the two for then there is some excuse there.

After supper I went out to look after chickens and dad was working down in the garden when he called to me and said something I did not hear. I called back and asked what he said. He would not answer me and I knew he got mad because I did not run down to see what he wanted. I finished my work and went in the house for I knew the storm would come. I did not just go when I ought to go because of people on every side. Well, I got to the house in time to ask the children if he had left any orders. They said he had not. Then he came and he told me I did not want to do anything, never did and that I would not let the children help him and that was the way things would be all summer and told me where I should go, of course. Wish I had a dollar for every time he has sent me below. We would not have to worry about the high cost of living. Of course, I don't mind if we are alone. Two nights ago he asked me to come down into the garden and help. Well, I went, of course, but had not been there five minutes when he started to rave. I walked to the house and never said a word. Guess he was sort of ashamed of himself. When he came up to the house he was nice the rest of the evening.

These spells come just so often and he thinks I ought to forget as soon as he does. I would not care if we were alone but I hate this kind of life so and it hurts. I can't help it. Of course, I don't want you to say anything about this to him. It only makes things worse but it gives you an idea of how things are run for just as sure as he has to work he gets

65

angry at everybody and everything and thinks he does it all. I don't see for my life how people can do business with him at times. Today at noon he said he had bought a lot of wheat and paid all it was worth. Now why does he buy grain that way and when it is so high. And that horse. Well I don't know what we are going to do with it and feed is so high. He will soon eat his head off.

Now dear don't let this bother you but I think you understand things better. I feel sorry for dad too for I don't think he can help it but it doesn't do his business any good.

This part of the letter is about the draft and possible army service in the war, which she calls, "this dirty business".

I am not sure that I wrote what I wanted to this afternoon or I made it understood for I had so little time to write but, of course, if you find that conditions at home will not let you remain then dad is right in wanting you to try now and I would rather you would do that then to be drafted later. Be sure and find this out first if you can. I have thought a little about Knute Nelson, if it would do any good to write him.

Can you find out for sure if this would keep you out of this dirty business? If not don't take any chances please on our account for we will manage some way.

I will send $25 soon as I get it if boys go home Fri. They well bring it Monday I hope and I will see that you get it soon as possible. Will also send the one shirt that dad brought in the morning and will wash the rest tomorrow.

The seniors play at Vining tonight. They were asked to come and at Underwood Saturday night.

It is late and the house is cold so must say good night and love from,

Mother

This letter shows the tensions that crop up in a marriage. Both Adsit and Louise were worried about paying the bills and exhausted from all the work at the store and at home. Adsit appears to have been hot tempered and Louise dared to stand up to him. Later, as Louise says, "the storm blew over" and they went back to their long lasting partnership.

Monday P.M. 1-19-19

Dear Charles, I wrote Clara, Sue and Hattie Sunday, so have you and
Agnes left. Shall write Agnes tonight—by the way we have not heard
from her for a long time, have you? Hope she is OK.

Dad has been very nice about showing me your letters and all has
been very peaceably for a long time. The storm was a big one but it
settled the dust for a while.

Snowed all day Sunday and rather wintery today. The children all
rode to school all right—This A.M. Mr. Hazelton took his team and
some kind of a rig and made a good road up to schoolhouse and many
other places. Very nice of him. I am sending you a lot of socks. I have
mended also the Christmas ones that Mrs. Smith made you. I rather
think you could use them now. Will send them off in A.M. as Edith is
going up now to let Dad come to coffee and try to fix the front door.

Lovingly, Mother

Dearest son,

Tuesday evening. Just a line before I go to bed. Just wrote a little to Sue
also as I had letter from Agnes to send over.

Everything is fine today. Everybody seems to be busy. John did not
want to go out today, so dad said, but he told him to go or he could not
keep him any longer. So he hiked although it was very cold and a lot of
snow but they still run the cows. Papa seems to think everything is O.K.
again. We had pancakes for breakfast. That helped get a good start. Well
it is so cold and everybody is in bed so guess I better go too.

Lovingly Mother

Thursday, 7:30 A.M.

Dear Charles- It seems the only time I have to write anymore is before the folks get-up. Dad and I just finished our breakfast and Bess, Leila and Hester are up. The rest are all in bed yet.

Will you be home Easter, April 4? How long? We have been going to church evenings extra meetings everywhere the last two weeks. Dad too and I guess it has done him some good. He is trying so hard to be good and really doing fine--long time since he went off about anything. Going to wash today so must close.
Lovingly, Ma

Wednesday, a.m.-7:15 2-25-20

This is rather early but it seems to be the only time I ever get to write. Just finished my breakfast and Dad has gone out to the barn and the rest are all in bed. Part of this letter is rather old but will send it anyway. School is closed this week. The town is full of the "Flu", no one very bad tho. Our boys went home Sat. so I'll be out a week on those. Cora B. too went home also forgot to pay her last—a bit hard on me. Mon. I'll send your yours when I get Mrs. Smith's check so you get yours. Roads very bad so business poor although not so very cold. Mrs. Smith is up again after three weeks in bed. Sue writes that she and Clara will be home last of March for awhile. Too bad Clara can't finish her short-hand. Sorry she even went but it cannot be helped.

Edith and I have been doing some painting this week while folks are gone—the hall and Sue's room upstairs.

Mrs. Smith was a long time boarder at the house and became very ill and needed constant care which was a huge burden on Louise. Clara went on to become a top notch secretary.

Monday Eve. (1920)

Dear Charles—Got box today. Thanks very much. Did you ever get that quilt? And do you want another one?

Uncle Ole died Saturday night about 11:30 but they did not call me till 6 in the morning for Edith and I were up Friday night till 4. I had to phone the folks and was kept busy all day. Never finished till after 6 P.M. Halverson was not here so they got the undertaker from Ottertail. Funeral will be Tues. at 1:00 P.M. at the Lutheran Church and Paulsen will be the pastor.

We washed today. It also snowed so clothes are all out tonight. Hope we don't get a storm. Very cold and wintery. Hope you will be able to get home next week.

Mr. and Mrs. John Hanson of Fergus Falls called here last evening. Mrs. H. said she was going to send Clara a box of candy for Thanksgiving. They seem very nice and pleased.

I told Holt to tell me when he got a crate of eggs but he must have forgotten. You will have to help Edith pack when you get here.

Dad was poorly last week but feels better now. Alice's address is Hosmer. We had letters last part of the week. I have been writing Agnes to come home. I am sure she needs a rest—and it will soon be a year since she has had a vacation.

Well there is nothing worth writing about so may as well stop.

Lovingly, Mother

Uncle Ole Stoa was Olea's brother and Louise's uncle.

The Hanson's were the parents of Dr. Elmer Hanson.
Clara and Elmer married in 1922.

Sunday 4/10/20

Dear Charles,

I wrote you a long letter a few days ago but found it this morning on the table so guess it is rather old now so will try again and see if I can get this one off.

Well we got a long letter from Agnes yesterday P.M. She seems to be getting along as well as she can expect. She speaks of coming home after awhile. It still keeps cold and we have a bit of snow every now and then so we don't forget winter. We washed a big washing Fri., cleaned storeroom and a lot more which left me with a stiff neck but it is letting go today so by Monday I'll be able to do anything.

Your shirting came, will try to make it soon, samples came also but they were no good. Hazelton sold his team so we bought some of his feed and hay, so the cow is doing much better.

This week we shall do some cleaning out of doors, tried to trim the grass yesterday but it did not work very well.

Suppose Dad writes you all the business news, and Len is here so Edith will write all about that or him. I must write the girls now so may God keep us all till we meet again.

Lovingly, Mother

Tuesday eve

Did not get my letter finished so will add a bit soon.

Edith is feeling better tonight. Seems Len was off hunting for a few days. He came down to ask her out in the car but it acted just the same as when I had it out. Something queer. It will not work on high. It just gets wild so he is going to take it up to Nelson tomorrow and see what that tinker did to it. Something about the fuel. Got some corn today. Say, did you know I have lost some chickens? That old yellow hen is gone for sure and the rest of the flock seems small. We got a big load of poles cut today and after school tonight Lorenzo piled it all on the back porch. He was so tired he cried. He thinks he had to do all the work you used to do. Today he asked me if I missed you anymore now that he worked so hard. Old Mrs. Herman was buried this afternoon. I did not have time to go tho. Well I won't be so busy after awhile if everybody quits school and things look very much that way now.

Lovingly, Mother

Edith married Len Langen in 1921.

11/8/22

Dear Charles,

I should have written before but it seemed too much like a funeral at first. Romper would lay up stairs in front of your door and wait for you to come out—I don't know what old George did at night. I could not hear him and in the day time he has to sleep.

Dad missed you too and is very proud of you. Well, I am glad you have work and wish you God's blessing and success. This P.M. Hattie and I went to United Aid. Yesterday, we voted and, of course, all came my way so I feel well paid for voting. We also got a lot of fun out of it. Mrs. Smith did not want to go so Miss Nelson, Hattie and I went and afterward we went downtown and met Mrs. Langen and she wanted me to go back with her. When we got there I found Mrs. Smith and asked her how it happened. She said Bundy came with his car and made her come but that I'd have to help her vote, so I took her right away from Mr. B. and he did look so funny. Just then J.B. gave him a poke in the side and the laugh was on Fred B. Everybody thought it the best thing for they all knew that vote was lost to their party.

It still rains when it doesn't snow but it all turns to water when it hits the ground. Sent your box today. Do you want your brown woolen shirt or anything else? So sorry we were slow in getting this off but this wet weather is bad.

Lovingly,
Mother

About the voting: Mrs. Smith, Louise's boarder, didn't want to go to vote but was later enticed into it with a ride from Mr. Bundy. And Louise is so pleased that she was able "to help her vote". This is two years after women won the right to vote.

Wednesday Eve

Dearest Charles--

Dad says come to bed and it is late too but somehow I feel as if I wanted just a wee visit with my boy. I wrote no Sunday letters. Have just finished one to Sue tonight. Very stormy today. Little children did not go to school at all.

I went to aid at Aldrich after school. Wanted to see their new house. Can't say I like it inside any better then I do the outside.

I got six eggs today. Shall send you some cake soon. It is so hard to get any work done with this cold weather.

Lorenzo had a birthday cake today. He thinks he is a very big boy now. Bessie is almost well and so is my back. Hattie got a diamond from George this week.

A good night and lots of love from Mother.

Harriet marred George Witthoft in 1928.

Sunday, A.M.

Dear Charles-

Thanks for the lovely plant- it came in fine shape. Mother's Day is a reminder of the sort of mother I am. Could I live my life over again with my little ones that were so dear to me, seems to me I could do better. I was so busy then with the cares of the day and not always as much to do with some but, that is no excuse to fail to do the work given one and yet I can see where I have failed in so many ways. May God forgive me and fill into your lives the things I failed to make good. I feel sorry for my mother who feels this as keenly as I do.

Raining a little tonight- rather cold.

Agnes called just after you did. She sent a doz. pink roses and check for $25. Alice sent check for $10. Clara sent lovely hose. Well I must get to work. Johnson promised me another week and surely there will be a change soon.

Lovingly, Mother

Olea Sahol, Louise's mother, died on Christmas Eve in 1924. She had been born on Christmas Eve in 1835.

Monday morning

Smith is still with us but has failed a lot the last 3 or 4 days. Can't help herself at all. I can only feed her milk or brandy with a teaspoon. She fights like mad as soon as I touch her.

We did not get the much needed rain—too cold I guess.

I am so sorry about the tax—strange we did not know. When should this have been paid?

Mrs. Smith died soon after this.

Adsit Hatch died in April 1929 of a stroke at age 73.

7/4/32

Dear Charles,

We had a note from Agnes a few days ago saying she was coming home in a week or ten days. I am looking for her about Sunday.

I visited Leila Sunday. Elmer and Clara took me over in the afternoon. She seems to be about the same—not much change.

Well, I as going to write and ask you something but it is too late to ask so will just tell you my plan. You perhaps remember the Ballmans, an old couple who stayed with me one summer long ago. Well they were very anxious to come back just for two weeks. I talked with Clara and Edith about it as they happened to be here at the time I got her letter. They both said, of course, I should take them. No one in the big room and too, it looked as if none of ours were coming home. So I wrote her to come. They expect to be here the Sunday eve of 14th. Yesterday she wrote again asking if she could bring her grandson and granddaughter. I did not know just what to do about this but I saw Mrs. Hanson and she will let them have rooms if I need any—so think I'll write and tell them to come. I am asking $10.00 per week. Over half will mean a profit for me and what is two weeks to compare with all winter with a house full of school children. I will not have to worry about my coal bills now. At least until after Christmas.

Hope you will not care. I shall get good help but just feel I need this extra to help out this fall. If the old man is still ambitious he will take care of the flowers and lawn. He worked like a hired man when here before.

Ren has the back building all down and is sorting lumber to be taken down here this P.M. I canned 10 qts of raspberries. I bought a crate. A lovely rain Mon. night but it's hot again today.

Jane sleeps most of the time—goes in swimming with Ren every afternoon.

Lovingly, Mother

Jane was the family bulldog.

Leila, Louise's niece, had tuberculosis and was in a sanitarium where she died in 1934.

After Adsit's death, Louise continued to rent out rooms. Charles took over the upkeep of the house and the rest of the children sent money when they could.

Thurs. P.M.

Dearest Charles,

I was indeed sorry to hear of your robbery and at this time of the year one needs so many clothes.

Ren is planning to go down but will use Kay's car as his is in the hospital again. He was worrying about all it would cost to get the thing fixed. In that case he will go over to Fergus Fri. night and they will start early Sat. A.M.

I went over to Fergus Tues. and paid the last half of the taxes which cleaned me up of all I had tried so hard to save and hang onto. But am so thankful I could and not let the thing go as we did last fall. Evelyn is leaving Mon. She has a better job and I cannot feed one extra anyway. I must manage some way of getting along without help.

Ren has been working hard at the wood pile also has most of the windows on. It has taken pounds of putty and some glass but they will be in good shape when done. Been very cold and I am trying to get along with only wood but it takes a lot to keep the house comfortable.

Went to a swell party Tues. at Rambergs (sweets and swells). Today I am invited to three places but, of course, can only go to one—it cuts into my time so but one must live too.

Lovingly, Mother

The Hatch house had its first indoor bathroom installed in 1924. Around 1943, Moma Lou's huge cast iron, wood burning stove and the wooden ice box were replaced with electric models. The kitchen hand pumps, attached to the well, were also removed, but the pump outside the kitchen door was there for years.

Mon. a.m.

Dearest Charles- Sorry I did not write before but every day is full. Last week we went out to two coffee parties. One at Dr. Berquist and one at Swenson. And one surprise party for John Lewis.

Well that is the way the times go, so fast, altho Sunday or the weekend I missed you so much.

Clara's folks were here last weekend. They are looking fine and in good spirits and Clara said you were just grand to her while she was in the city. She raved about you and Ren--what grand men you both were. She never seemed to see so much good in anyone before except Elmer. I have heard so many grand things about my boys and girls of late when I am out—that I begin to think I have quite a swell family.

About Duke that stuff did the business but now my trouble is what to feed him. He is always hungry and crying for more food. He eats me out of house and home!

Storm windows on but the cost! I pd. them Sat. We should have a new lumberman here ($31.65). Cold and freezing everynight. That is the water in the chicken pens. Still burning wood but must get coal soon-this week. Yesterday Ren was married 2 years-wonder if he will be up over the weekend.

Shall be happy to see you Thurs.

Lovingly,
Mother

Ren married Katharine Bell in 1938.

Sunday P.M. 2/28/43

Dearest Charles—Thank you for the letter and check. Glad Feb. is going out. It has been a hard month. Snowing hard right now and walking is bad. Did not dare go to church this morning.

Had letter from Bud Bell. He seemed quite happy and in good spirits.

Also had letter from Warren Fri., seemed rather blue and is suffering a lot with his feet—poor boy.

Donald has the measles at least that's what the Dr. called it. Have all three children in this weekend. We took out the oil heater as it smoked so much and then too we had used up our oil. The little laundry stove works fine.

Will let you know later how things are coming.

Lovingly,
Mother

Bud Bell was Ren's brother-in-law. He was in the Navy during the war and was always welcomed at the house. Warren was a friend of Charlie's, who was in the Army.

Donald and the children were boarders.

Mon. P.M.
1/11/45

Dearest Charles, Thank you so much for helping make Christmas what it was—It was all very lovely I thought.

Thank you also for the gifts. Snowing again as I look out. Yesterday was grand but I was kept busy wiping up the back porch for that roof will leak.

I have not heard from Alice since she left but know she will be busy because she was late—left here the day her school opened. While here, Alice renewed her membership to the church and left a check for herself and one for little Susan K.'s membership. It made me very happy and I hope some more of you will see the need of this in the near future. After all we and our boys are fighting for what we have turned our backs on or neglected. Hope and pray this year will be one of "back to the church and our God" for we never know when Christ will come or when we will be called.

God bless you,
Lovingly Mother

Owen Langen, Louise's grandson and the son of Edith and Len Langen, was killed on April 21, 1945 in Okinawa during World War II. He was 22 years old. Owen was a scholar and an athlete. He went to the University of Missouri to study journalism and wanted to be a writer. He was a young man greatly admired and loved by everyone who knew him.

Nov. 21/45

Dearest Charles--Another cold nasty day, air full of snow.

The Langens will be here tomorrow. Have not heard from Dorothy wonder what she plans to do. If Sue is going to Chicago we may drive down with Rack sometime next week.

That *will* Charles has given me much pain and grief. I hate to say this but you know it is not as it should be. I don't want to make the same mistake that so many others have made. I must be fair to all and I know you too want to keep the love and respect of all including the little ones Tommy, Susan, Steve and all the rest. This cannot and will not be if that will holds. It will split the family forever and for so little! Is it worth it?

We must always look at a thing from the other person's viewpoint to be fair. Just read it and put Ren's name or one of the girls in your place and see what you think of it in that light. You all have enough to live in comfort, may we also live in peace!

I don't want it said when I am gone that I blundered too in giving all to one. When that will was made I had no money saved. I had put it all in paying bills and repairing the home and other buildings. I have denied myself many comforts and things in order to leave a little to all, that is only right—as it has come from all. I know you have done more work than most of them but that does not count in this as much as this has been self inflicted and much of it will benefit you in the future. The girls all worked hard while at home and received nothing when they left. So may God help me and help you to see this as I do before it is too late. The keys and Round Robin matters not as compared to this in holding the family together.

Lovingly, Mother

Nov. 25, '45

Dearest Charles--You got me all wrong or misunderstood what I was trying to say in regards to that will. First, you know I never intend or could give the home to be cared for to anyone but you. I said read the will with some other name in the place of yours and see if from that viewpoint you would think all was right. Maybe I have not made it all clear yet. To look at a thing from all sides is the thing to do and I want to do all things for the best of all so God help me.

I showed the will to Sue and she did not think it would do much to hold the family together and that some would never come home. Of course, there is not much chance it would be sold but why, if it is, should three have over ½--that is the three of you and that does not look right to me either. Agnes does not need more than the others. Hester has and always will put as much into the home as the rest. Some cannot and that is not their fault. They were given no chance after they finished high school. I dare say some would have gone far had they had the chance of the older ones. You say I have changed. Yes, my dear one I have—but not for the better but this comes not to me alone. We all grow old and are not wanted. I have felt this for a long time that I am only in the way—of no account any more which is true. May God grant I shall not continue here much longer. My work is finished and I am waiting to move on. The only hard part of it is I feel keenly I have failed my God and my children.

What more can I say? I am only trying to avoid what others did before me as Lena, Father and Mother, Uncle Allen and Charles Adsit and I could name so many. It is late but I shall mail this tonight.

Lovingly, Mother

Louise left the house to Charles when she died in 1968 and Charles left it in a trust for his nephews and nieces when he died in 1973. Here Louise mentions inequities that occur in a family and how some of the children had an advantage because of education and others through marriages. At age 74 Louise sadly says her work is finished.

Sunday eve.   (Spring 1940's)

Dearest Charles--Thank you for the lovely lily-it is beautiful. There are five blossoms open today. Also thank you for everything while I was in the city. The Wittbeckers were over for coffee this afternoon. It rains all the time, sorry we did not start raking the lawn before, it is so heavy and wet. Warren has this cold that is going around so cannot drive him very hard. May have to get Erickson to help if the rain ever lets up. I had to wait one and a half hours in Staples. Found everything O.K. when I got here only poor Kee Poo had missed me dreadfully. Loraine said she tried to comfort her by picking her up but she would go all over the house and just howl and she would not let me get out of her sight the first few days. Erickson had the fence moved and most of the spading done when I came home. Helen and Art came and we drove to the cemetery and also around town for a little while this afternoon.

Mrs. Anderson is visiting in Henning. I let her know before she left that we would want her room for the summer. She was not at all pleased about it but hope she will feel better when she gets back. Mrs. Swenson wants Lorraine but cannot take her till the end of this month and asked me please to keep her till she can make room for her. Otherwise she will go to Mrs. H. Larson so I think I'll keep her.

Found letter from Alice when I got home with check for $25.00 to buy nails for the house. That ought to nail it up tight. I have set quite a few of the plants out on the porch but shall watch if it gets cold. I can take them in for a day or so.

Good night and God bless you,
Lovingly,
Mother

After a visit to Minneapolis, Louise gave a rundown on the boarders. She needed to have rooms free for the summer when her family came home.
Helen was Louise's niece, Lena's daughter, who lived in town.
Kee-Poo was a sleek black cat that Louise loved dearly and ruled the house.
Louise did not like to travel but made the effort to visit her children's homes to please them over the years. She got terribly homesick and was always so happy be back at her old house.

Thurs. a.m. 1/25/46

Dearest Charles--Well everyday brings us that much nearer to spring and am I glad! I cannot see that it helps much to close off part of the house. The result is only frozen water pipes and cold feet and I do not believe we have saved anything on fuel.

The dog and cats eat me out of house and home. Old "Pouts" can eat as much as Duke any day—he has just moved in to stay. I bake cornbread for them and give them milk, of course. Kee-poo must have her food. Sue and Rack were over for coffee one Sunday not long ago and she has called too to see how we are.

Oh, yes, no it was not the cesspool. We thought it must be as Joe could not find a thing only that it would not go down—so Mon. A.M. I had Erickson come down and expected to start digging a new pool but I thought of one more place and had him cut out a piece in the floor in the little hallway and there we found the pipe encased in heavy ice. I used boiling water on it and after a few hot pots of water "plunk" down it went—no more trouble there since we packed it well with rags. Then the pipe in the basement was next, two mornings later but I could fix that. The poor H.'s dog these cold days makes my heart ache. I cannot love such people, their cat too. They will suffer for this I know—some day they ought to. Hope he will freeze his front off when he comes home to dinner.

Yes, by all means get some bulbs. You have not enough! You could use a few 1,000,000 down in the potato garden for nothing else grows there anyway.

Did you go to church Sun? Don't be a communist or a "new dealer" or a Red or something God doesn't want you to be.

Lovingly,
Mother

There were no sewers in the town and each house had its own septic tank. The pipes froze often in the winter and when neither Joe, a relative, nor Erickson, the plumber, could help solve her problem, Louise figured out what to do on her own.
The mistreated neighbor's dog, Wimpy, soon found a happy and permanent home at the Hatch house.

83

Income, Insurance, Policies   1950

THURSDAY, JUNE 15

A bad wind storm about 6: P.M.
uprooted the big tree where all
the birds had their houses.

Daddy planted this tree in
June 1894 almost 56 years to the day
when it came down. Everything
looked bad Trees down on all sides and
the lights were off so Tommy & Susan
& I had a cold supper. God knew
we needed help so he sent Chas.
home to take over.

FRIDAY, JUNE 16

A crew of boys & men are
working cleaning up the place
We plan to replant the big tree
with top and most of its branches
gone it may take root again.

The Children have been
busy picking up dead birds
all day – a sad sight. Many barns
went down and cattle killed out
in county. Sue was over this P.M.
and little Susan went back with her.

84

1950

From the date book of Louise Hatch

Thursday, June 15

A bad wind storm about 6 P.M. uprooted the big tree where all the birds had their houses.

Daddy planted this tree in June 1894 almost 56 years to the day when it came down. Everything looked bad, trees down on all sides and the lights were off so Tommy & Susan & I had a cold supper. God knew we needed help so he sent Chas home to take over.

A crew of boys & men are working cleaning up the place.

We plan to to plant the big tree with top and most of its branches gone it may take root again.

The children have been busy picking up dead birds all day – a sad sight – many homes went down and cattle killed out in country. Sue was over this P.M. and little Susan went back with her.

Susan and Tom Hatch were visiting their grandmother during this storm. The top of the large elm tree, re-planted in the center of the yard, took root and sixty years later is taller than ever. Charles made dozens of birdhouses with his nephews and nieces which were hung in all the trees in the yard.

Saturday August 6 – 1960

And this is the day poor old Rocky was put to sleep he is now resting under the old lilac tree back of the garage

Joe, Alice and I were in Fergus that P.M.

Battle Lake Minn.
Sept. 25, '63

Dearest Mary,

I was so happy to receive your letter card. I thought you had forgotten me and B.L.

Yes, I think it would be nice if you get married at Christmas time providing you can find a man good enough for you and then you could visit B.L. on your honeymoon. I'd like to meet the one you would tie to for *life*. He'd better be good or he will have a tough old great grandmother in-law to deal with. Better tell him I was born in 1871. Can you figure that far back?

Well we just had our P.M. coffee on the back porch. A beautiful day. I went with Charles out into the country for a ride, he had some business to take care of.

No frost yet, our flowers and garden are still nice. We enjoy corn every evening for dinner.

I am looking forward to your mother coming home in October (hunting time). Harriet is in Fergus helping Sue. I hope she comes home today. End of my paper so will take a walk in garden.

God bless you and love.

Grama Lou

Louise wrote this to her granddaughter, Mary Shepard Phillips, when she was 92.

Thursday P.M. Oct. 10, '63

Dearest Dorothy, Thank you much for the surprise gift that I found in my desk. I just finished a pair of booties for Steve Jr. I'll send them to you to forward for I am not sure of his address. It was so wonderful to see you and thanks a lot for all the nice rides we had. It rained this morning and is dark and may rain again. Letter from Agnes. Chas is going up for P.M. mail so all for now.

God Bless you and love,

Mother

Feb. 21 – '64

Dearest Dorothy

Charles in city – been there all week – expect him back next Sunday.

A beautiful day, not much snow left and it is going fast. Been rather a lonely winter – so many of my neighbors gone and I can not go outside, with the help of the cane I can get around in the house.

Shall soon start cleaning up the back porch so can put on my coat and sit out there. Poor Mrs. Swenson is in Elbow Lake and I am afraid she will never come back to her home. Her eyes are failing and in her letter she said everything was turning black and her letter was hard to make out. She has no one that can come and live with her but she is so homesick for her little house and Battle Lake. Old age is hard to take for all!!

God bless you and your loved ones.

Mother

Louise was a great knitter. She made beautiful sweaters and afghans and made a pair of baby booties for each of her great grandchildren.
Hannah Swenson was Louise's oldest friend who lived in the house on the other side of her garden.

88

Sunday P.M. 3 – 15 – 64

Dearest Bessie,

Thank you for the letter and gift. A beautiful day although there is a little cold wind. Sue was over and took me for a long ride. Charles is in the city for almost all week. Hope he gets home soon.

The children are so busy playing outside now, that they don't have much time to come in. Danny was worried....where would the fish live now that they have taken all the fish houses off the lake?

Our snow is almost all gone and things begin to have a green look....a good rain would be nice about this time.

Am so anxious to get the back porch cleaned up and put in order for our coffee parties.

Later. I took a little walk and now it will soon get dark, altho the days are getting longer. Time to go as I hear the supper going on the table.

Thank you again and God bless you and yours,

Love,

Mother

The children were, Bobby, Ricky and 3 year old Danny Hanson, Louise's great-grandchildren who lived across the street.
Charlie had a live-in aide to help his mother.

Coming to America

Coming to America

Louise and her family came to America in 1881 when she was nine years old. Her father, Hans, was a second son and inherited only a small plot of land in Norway to farm. He also was a cabinet maker and Louise's mother, Olea, was a midwife. Making a living was difficult and they decided their children would have a better future abroad. They packed up their belongings in trunks and traveled first to Bergen and then to England before making the long crossing over the Atlantic. The family consisted of the parents, two sons, Anders and Ole, and four daughters, Olena, Louise, Helga and Karen. They used the surname Sahol, which was the name of the family farm in Honefoss. Hans had also used the name Evjen, meaning inlet, which may have designated his smaller farm. They arrived at Castle Clinton in New York to pass through immigration and were not allowed to continue their journey because Karen was ill. She was taken by a horse drawn ambulance to a hospital and Hans, not understanding English or knowing where she was going, followed on foot and stayed with her until she was fit to travel. The family then reunited and set off by train for Ashby, Minnesota. There they met Olea's brothers, Theodore and Ole Stoa, who had acquired land for the family in Otter Tail County on Silver Lake about 30 miles north. Hans and the older children went on to the property, by wagon, leaving the young girls with relatives. It is said that the Sahols were taken aback when they saw their new farm, which was full of trees and rocks and on a lake shore. Olea asked her brother, Theodore, why he had chosen that land and he told her that it had reminded him of their place in Norway. It was a homestead without suitable fields and they had to work very hard to create a farm. They built a house, cleared the land and planted crops. Months later, Louise was given a wagon ride over to Silver Lake to meet her parents. There were no roads, so when they were near the Sahol property, she was left off to run up a hill, through dense, tall prairie grass. She bravely made her way to find her surprised family and a very happy reunion.

Ellis Island did not exist at the time the Sahols immigrated, however Louise Sahol Hatch's name is registered there on a plaque, to make note of her journey to a new life.

M.S.P.

Baptismal Certificate
August 15, 1872
Norway

Kokoppe-Indpodnings-Attest.

Louise Hansdatter Sahol

Louise Hansdatter Sohol

født i *Hole* af Forældrene *Gf*

Hans Halvorsen og Gift Olea An-
Hans Halvorson   Olea An-

dersdatter og boende i *Hole*
    dersdatter

1 Aar gammel, er af mig Underskrevne, Aar
1872 den *1ste August* indpodet med Kokopper. Ved nøi-
agtigt Eftersyn imellem den 7de og 9de Dag efter Indpodningen
har jeg fundet alle de Tegn, som vise dem at være de ægte Kokopper: de vare nemlig hele og ubestabigede, opfyldte med en klar
Bædste, i Midten nedtrykkede, og omgivne med en rød Cirkel;

Louise Hansdatter
Louise Hansdatter

har da ordentlig gjennemgaaet de ægte Kokopper, som beskytte
for Børnekopper; hvilket herved, paa Ære og Samvittighed,
bevidnes af

Haudstad den *15 August* Aar *1872.*

Ole Harum

In Norway at that time, boys were given their father's name with son added as in Hans Halvorson, son of Halvor. Daughters were given their father's name with datter added as in Olea Andersdatter, daughter of Anders and Louise Hansdatter, daughter of Hans. Sahol is also included on the certificate as a surname. Louise was baptized at Bonseness Church in Ringerike. The certificate is issued from the nearby town of Hole.

Kokoppe-Indpodnings-Attest.

Louise Hansdatter Sohol

født i *Hole* af Forældrene *Gt*
Hans Halvorsen og hans Olea An-
derisdatter og boende i *Hole*
1 Aar gammel, er af mig Underskrevne, Aar
1872 den *7de August* indpodet med Kokopper. Ved nøi-
agtigt Eftersyn imellem den 7de og 9de Dag efter Indpodningen
har jeg fundet alle de Tegn, som vise dem at være de ægte Kokopper: de vare nemlig hele og ubestadigede, opfyldte med en klar
Vædste, i Midten nedtrykkede, og omgivne med en rød Cirkel;

Louise Hansdatter

har da ordentlig gjennemgaaet de ægte Kokopper, som beskytte
for Bornekopper; hvillet herved, paa Ære og Samvittighed,
bevidnes af

Haandstad den *15de August* Aar *1872*.

Ole Hanum

The Sahol Family
Ole, Anders, Lena, Louise,
Olea, Hans, Helga
Karen died in 1885

Olea and Hans Sahol

The Sahol Farm
Ringerike Norway

To
Louise Hatch
from
Mother

I submit you to God and
His word of grace that is mighty
to lift you up and give you your
birthright among the holy.

*Inscription in the Bible of Louise Sahol Hatch,
written by her mother, Olea Sahol in Norwegian.*

The Statue of Liberty-Ellis Island Foundation, Inc.

proudly presents this

Official Certificate of Registration

in

THE AMERICAN IMMIGRANT WALL OF HONOR

to officially certify that

Louise Sahol Hatch

came to the United States of America from

Norway

joining those courageous men and women who came to this country in search of personal freedom, economic opportunity and a future of hope for their families.

Lee A. Iacocca
The Statue of Liberty-Ellis Island
Foundation, Inc.

A. C. Hatch

Adsit C. Hatch (1855-1929)

Adsit was born on a farm in Dane County Wisconsin in 1855. Both his mother, Elizabeth Adsit, and his father, Lorenzo Hatch, were from families that first came to New England in the 1700's from England and steadily migrated west. Adsit graduated from Albion Academy and earned a teaching degree before setting out for an adventure in Texas. There he suffered a leg injury which bothered him for the rest of his life. Around 1880 he came to Minnesota with the idea of studying law with Knute Nelson, a family friend and later Governor and Senator from Minnesota. Instead, Adsit became one of the founding fathers of the new town of Battle Lake. He went into business, eventually owning a brick yard, a hardware and implement store and a grain elevator. At his implement company he sold wagons, buggies, vehicles, power machines, cream separators, pumps, pipes, windmills and lightning rods. He was a founder and the first president of Hardware Mutual Insurance Company of Minnesota and served as a director of the company for many years.

Adsit built a house, married, and had a daughter Libby. His wife died suddenly in 1884, and he hired Louise Sahol to care for his daughter. Louise and Adsit were married in 1890 and had 12 children. Five of the children had their father's bright red hair.

Adsit was an innovative enterpreneur and a prosperous and successful businessman for 35 years. However, by 1915, he began having financial problems. The brickyard closed with the advent of machine-made bricks, and a competing hardware store opened in town. Louise complains in her letters that while the farmers were doing well, they didn't pay their bills on time and Adsit's accounts were often behind. The buying of grain always entailed financial risks.

Fishing and baseball were two of Adsit's favorite pastimes. Because of his leg he couldn't play ball but was the manager of the local team for years. He was also mayor or Battle Lake and on the school board. He was a longtime Justice of the Peace for the village. During one of the great grasshopper invasions, he helped save the day and the crops by improvising a huge machine, called a hopper-dozer. Made of sheet iron and using kerosene, it disposed of 32,000 bushels of the insects.

Active in politics, he worked on Nelson's campaigns which were very hard fought. A great reader, Adsit was said to have had one of the largest private libraries in Otter Tail County. His book shelf suggests that Dickens was his favorite author. In April of 1929, Adsit died of a stroke at age 73. A letter from his friend, Senator Nelson, written a few years earlier, summed up Adsit's life: "While you've had your ups and downs in business you are still on earth and doing business at the old stand. Though you may not die a millionaire, you will die with the consciousness that you have done some good in the world and brought up such a nice family of children."

M.S.P.

In 1898 Adsit went to the hospital in Brainerd to have an operation on his leg, which he injured in Texas as a young man. He had the surgery in February and had to stay six weeks for recovery. This was very hard on Louise who had to take care of the children, the house, and the animals as well as keeping an eye on the hardware store. Adsit walked with a limp for the rest of his life.

Brainerd   March 7   3 O'clock
My Dear Wife,

Leg dressed yesterday. My foot and leg below knee are stronger and I feel first rate today. I have been out walking today, walked as far as from the house to the store. It is very warm and pleasant, nearly all the boys are outside today. Before noon I played checkers, beat the old champion 3 games. Came out 3 games ahead. Also played whist. There are but 2 now confined to their bed in our ward and it is very lonesome w/o them. I'm going to read this afternoon.

Well I suppose tomorrow is the great day in Battle Lake. I wish I were there but I hope my vote will not be needed. I would feel bad if it won by only 1 vote. Our minister practiced a fierce sermon yesterday. There is a very sick man in private room upstairs.

Now dear Louise, don't worry. I am getting along finely and not so homesick as I was Friday and Saturday. I shall write to the little folks. I have nothing more to write unless I tell you how much love I have for you and how much you are in my thoughts which you will know.

With best love.
Your husband A C

4 O'clock

We have just rec a new patient in ward and he is an Irish engineer. He is a great joker, he has a tumor, but he has kept the whole ward laughing for some time.

You say I must be home soon as you can't get along without me. Well, dear, if I can get along here you certainly ought to do first rate at home with all the darlings to comfort you. If I could only see one of the kids it would help me out greatly. Well dear, I shall be home sometime before long, then we will be the happiest family in Minnesota.
I take lots of comfort looking forward to that time.
Give all the kids a kiss for papa.

With great love,
Your Husband

Adsit C. Hatch

Adsit as a young man

Papa with Alice, Dorothy, Edith, Clara, Bessie

Daddy Ad and Ren

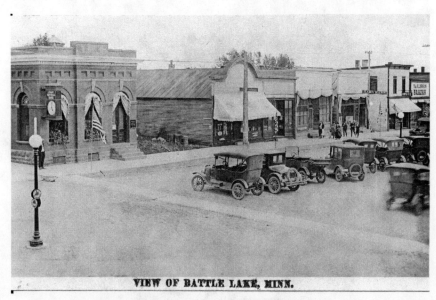

Hatch Hardware Store – fifth building from left

KNUTE NELSON, MINNESOTA, CHAIRMAN.
WILLIAM P. DILLINGHAM, VT.
FRANK B. BRANDEGEE, CONN.
WILLIAM E. BORAH, IDAHO.
ALBERT B. CUMMINS, IOWA.
LE BARON B. COLT, R. I.
THOMAS STERLING, S. DAK.
GEORGE W. NORRIS, NEBR.
RICHARD P. ERNST, KY.
SAMUEL M. SHORTRIDGE, CALIF.

CHARLES A. CULBERSON, TEX.
LEE S. OVERMAN, N. C.
JAMES A. REED, MO.
HENRY F. ASHURST, ARIZ.
JOHN K. SHIELDS, TENN.
THOMAS J. WALSH, MONT.

SIMON MICHELET, CLERK.

United States Senate,
COMMITTEE ON THE JUDICIARY.

Jan. 25, 1923.

Hon. A. C. Hatch,
Battle Lake, Minn.

Dear Friend:

Your very interesting letter of the 18th, with newspaper clipping, came to hand. Yes, all the members of that committee to which you refer are dead, except yourself and Comstock. Comstock is still alive, but in very feeble condition, I am informed. McCrea died years ago. Gilman is very feeble and cannot last very long, as he is now about 90 years of age. Kindred died about two years ago. He had lost his wife some years previously.

That was a wonderful convention, and it resulted in a red hot campaign. I never worked harder in my life than I did then. The railroads were few in the district; there were no automobiles, and it was a job to get around. I held meetings all over the district as far as I could reach. I was out nearly two months, and when the campaign was over, I was utterly exhausted. It took me over a month to get shipshape again.

You rendered me great service in that campaign which I shall never forget. You are very fortunate in having raised such a fine family, and while you have had your ups and downs in business affairs, you are still on earth and doing business at the old stand. Though you may not die a millionaire, you will die with the consciousness that you have done some good in the world and brought up such a nice family of children.

I did not know before that you had been teaching school up at Spring Prairie.

You must try and get acquainted with Gov. Preus. He is a chip off the old block, and a very good and reliable man.

As for myself, you have, of course, heard that I lost my wife last summer, and you know that my daughter made an unfortunate marriage. I am living here with a housekeeper, a widow woman fifty-four years old, a niece of my wife; and I am getting along fairly well. Ida is at home. She has been planning to go to California but the last report I had was that instead of going to California, she is going to Battle Creek.

112

KNUTE NELSON, MINNESOTA, CHAIRMAN.
WILLIAM P. DILLINGHAM, VT.   CHARLES A. CULBERSON, TEX.
FRANK B. BRANDEGEE, CONN.   LEE S. OVERMAN, N. C.
WILLIAM E. BORAH, IDAHO.   JAMES A. REED, MO.
ALBERT B. CUMMINS, IOWA.   HENRY F. ASHURST, ARIZ.
LEBARON B. COLT, R. I.   JOHN K. SHIELDS, TENN.
THOMAS STERLING, S. DAK.   THOMAS J. WALSH, MONT.
GEORGE W. NORRIS, NEBR.
RICHARD P. ERNST, KY.
SAMUEL M. SHORTRIDGE, CALIF.
SIMON MICHELET, CLERK.

United States Senate,

COMMITTEE ON THE JUDICIARY.

Hon. A. C. Hatch.....2

     In a few days I shall fill my eightieth year. I am fairly
well, considering my advanced years, and am still able to do a
fair amount of work, although I do not talk as often in the sen-
ate as I used to, and find I have to keep more quiet. My mind
is as good as ever, but I get tired quicker and find a necessity
for conserving my vitality as much as possible.

     If we adjourn the fourth of March, so that we can stay at
home the coming summer, I shall make it a point to come up and
visit you. I believe a niece of my aunt, Mrs. Kvilekval, who
married a Mr. Scott, is now on the old place, and she has invited me to come and visit her. She stayed with my aunt many
years before she died. You probably know her.

     With my best wishes to you and your family, I remain

          Yours, truly,

          Knute Nelson

Mementos

January, 1906.   January, 1906.

SUN. 18 / 18-347   SUN. 22 / 53-312

Shoes for   1906.

MON. 19 / 19-346   Jan. 8.   MON. 2? / 26-33?

Prune   one   pair U.S. 31 . 75

TUES. 20 / 20-345   Feb. 28   Hatti   No. 12. 1.2?   TUES. 27 / 27-33?

March 16. Susie   " 3½. 2.10

WED. 21 / 21-344   " "   20. Agnes   " 4 . 1.75   WED. 28 / 128-337
" "   25. Charle Rub. "   . 60
" "   30. Susie   " "   "   . 60
" "   " " Agnes   " "   . 50

THUR. 22 / 22-343   April 30. Irene   3½   .95   THUR. 29 / 2?-3?6
May 28 Edith shoe 7½   1.25
June 1   Charle slipper 13½   1.50

rent for in may
FRI. 23 / 23-842   for Alice   7   .50   FRI. 30 / 30-355
Clara   8   .50
Irene   3½   .35
Clara June 1.   7½   1.00

SAT. 24 / 24-841   July 4 pair of slippers   SAT. 31 / 31-334
Susie   Agnes   Hattie Edith about 4. 00

January 1906

Shoes for 1906

Child's name, dates and prices paid for shoes

117

WHOOPING COUGH REMEDY

Mix one lemon sliced,
1 cup whole flax seed,
2 oz comb honey,
One quart water.

Let simmer, not boil for four hours, Then strain. If less than a pint add
water to make one pint. Dose: one tablespoonful three times a day and
after each coughing spell. Guaranteed to cure in four days if taken when
child first whoops.

Whooping Cough Remedy.

Mix one lemon sliced, 1 oz. whole flax seed, 2 ounces comb honey, one quart water. Let simmer, not boil, four hours, then strain. If less than a pint add water to make one pint. Dose, one tablespoonful three times a day and after each coughing spell. Guaranteed to cure in four days if taken when child first whoops.

Louise in 1935 on a trip to Norway with her daughter, Alice.

June 16, 1935 left for Europe
Sept " 1930 " " Fergus Falls
Nov. " 1886 I came to the place
I call home
16 must be my ? number

Left England July 16 for
Norway
and
Left Antwerp Bel. Aug 16 for
home

Mrs. Hatch Tells of Interesting Sights On Trip Through Old Norway

Local Woman and Daughter Tell of Many Interesting Sights On Their Voyage.

Oslo, Norway,
August 2, 1935

To the Editor of the Review and our friends and relatives at home:

We are now in the lovely and hospitable land of the Midnight Sun. To have the sunlight with us at all hours is an experience never to be forgotten.

We left England on the Norwegian boat "Venus" and arrived in Bergen the following morning. The entrance into Bergen was a most impressive one. We sailed far into a fiord before we reached the dock. The mountains rose high above us on either side.

After a short stay in Bergen we left by train for Oslo. This trip is considered one of Norways most scenic trips. We rode in the valleys by the waters edge and climbed mountains so high we looked out on banks of snow and down on the tops of great tall pine forests. We climbed to such heights that the pressure on our ea rdurms was like that in an airplane. We went throuhg tunnels made longer by great snow sheds built over the entrances and exits.

All along the way we saw an abundance of flowers and every farm, no matter how small seemed to possess an orchard and a flower garden. We saw many old and quaint places but just as many prosperous and modern ones.

MAMA LOU'S FRUITCAKE
Battle Lake, Minnesota

1 cup brown sugar
1 " butter
1 " molasses
1 " sweet milk
3 " flour
4 eggs
3 level teaspoons baking P.
2 pounds of raisins
1 " " currants
1 Tea. S. cloves 1 of nutmeg
1 " " cinnamon
Juice of one lemon and one
orange it also calls for ½ pound
of citron but I get a few boxes of
any candied or fruit all prepared
in little boxes - it matters not
how much you put in
Bake 4 hours in slow oven

Louise with her bulldogs, Jane and Duke

Mama Lou on her back porch

And with her hollyhocks

From Mother Lou's Bible

St. Mathew	5: 3-12
	5: 21-24
Psalms	19, 14
	91, 23, 121, 20
Acts	3: 19
	4: 11-12

Psalm 146.
  "   23.
  "   51: 10–11.
St John, 14: 1–6.
  "   14: 13–14–15.
  "   14: 27.
  "   17: 7–26.
John, 1: 7.
2 Peter 3: 10,
Ephesians 4: 30–32.

MEMORIAL SERVICES

FOR

Mrs. A. C. (Louise) Hatch

BIRTH: June 29, 1871   DEATH: January 3, 1968

SERVICES AT
First Lutheran Church
Battle Lake, Minnesota

MONDAY, JANUARY 8, 1968 — 2:00 p.m.

CLERGY
Rev. Wesley Haugen

MUSIC
Mrs. Arvid Swedberg of Fergus . . Vocal
"Rock of Ages"
"Lead Kindly Light"
Mrs. Leonard Olson . . . . . Organist

PALLBEARERS

Glenn Johnson	Richard Hanson
Art Haga	Ralph Newman
Clifford Pederson	Edmund Everts

INTERMENT
First Lutheran Church Cemetery
Battle Lake, Minnesota

Arrangements by
NILSON FUNERAL HOME
Battle Lake, Minnesota

A Granddaughter's Memories

Spring 2009

Memories of Grandma Lou

Written by Susan Hatch Devine (I was the oldest of four children, born in 1941, of Grandma Lou's 12th child, Lorenzo Rexford Hatch. My brother, Tom, born in 1943, and I spent two weeks during many summers in Battle Lake. It would have been during the late 1940's and probably ended in 1952 for me. Grandma Lou would have been in her late seventies and even early 80's. She was slowing down, didn't bake and cook like she once did, but was a very wise, loving women who made a very important impact on my life.)

My siblings and I called her Grandma and Grandma Lou as we got older. Other grandchildren and extended family fondly referred to her as Gramma Lou or Mama Lou. I remember her in many settings.........................one of the earliest was as she sat in a rocker, or was it an overstuffed chair, placed near the heat register in the front room. She would be knitting, even with her crippled rheumatoid fingers using every scrap of yarn to knit booties, mittens etc. for family members or poor families living in dilapidated houses outside Battle Lake. I still have my booties which were knit for my adult feet..............primarily blue but with red, white, grey and black yarn. I only have a couple of things of hers and they are amongst the dearest things I own.

I remember Uncle Charlie (her oldest son) driving Grandma, myself and probably my brother Tom out into the country to deliver knit items and other supplies to a family living in a house with broken windows. I felt humbled as we drove away that day. I was aware that she took care of other families as well with her meager resources.

One prominent memory of mine occurred when Tom and I were visiting Grandma by ourselves. While Tom and I were pretending to be Indians and intending to walk all around Battle Lake, the sky began darkening and the wind "came up." We hurried back to the house to find that the three of us could barely get the front door shut. The resulting tornado uprooted the beautiful old tree next to the house and thankfully missed us. During all of this I remember a calm, strong grandmother..............

she must have been fearful with the responsibility of two young children but never showed it.

Another unforgettable experience occurred when Tom and I were visiting Grandma along with the Shepards which included Aunt Dorothy, Uncle Bob, Sally, Mary, Steve, and Bill. It was during the polio scare and before there was a vaccination for the dreaded-disease. Tom became very ill with a high fever and terrible pain in his legs. He was unable to walk. I remember him resting on the sofa in the parlor while Grandma baked huge onions, wrapped them and placed them along his legs. Polio, which was very contagious, was the fear so we children were told to play outside during the day and our parents were called in Des Moines, Iowa where we lived. The following adventure involved a private plane and pilot my parents flew in from Iowa, delay in getting Tom out due to weather, a landing in a field near St. Cloud due to airplane trouble and finally a hospital in Des Moines. Tom had rheumatic fever, another dreaded disease. He suffered some long term damage and had to learn to walk again. The doctors praised Grandma Lou's treatment of baked onions as moist heat was a good short term therapy. I suspect that she had deferred to her mother's training as a mid-wife when she came up with that idea.

I remember her sitting at the dining room table having political discussions with Gerry Bissinger (Aunt Hester's husband) in particular. I don't remember the views expressed but know she stated her own knowledgeable opinions clearly and with conviction. I guess the Battle Lake Review must have had some limited national and world news in it. I've since learned she also read the Fergus Journal everyday. And, of course, the radio could have been a resource although I don't remember it ever turned on. At that same table she taught me to play Nine Men Morris and all of the strategies she used. I had to work very hard to beat her which didn't happen often.

It was a special treat when the house nearly burst with the presence of other aunts, uncles and cousins. At dinner time when they were there, the women would help Grandma Lou start dinner, and then they would gather with the men in the "barn". Grandma Lou didn't allow alcohol in the house so the adults found this rickety old structure for their social time. In the barn was a worn out pump organ, a true ice chest, a motley assortment of old chairs and some fun loving adults. We children were not included, but we frequently heard loud, raucous, laughter erupt. I think it was 6:00 pm or maybe 6:30 pm when Grandma Lou would ring a bell from the porch outside her room and the adults would begin to gather in the house. We sat in the longest table on the big screened in- porch outside the kitchen. Over the years that porch has some how shrunk and could not possibly have held the long table in my memory. Grandma Lou always sat at the head of the table with Charlie at her left. Dinner would begin after we said grace.

If it was in season, we were treated to Uncle Charlie's homegrown corn. We children would be sent down to the back garden to collect a bag of corn after the water had started boiling in the kitchen. (That corn didn't need butter; it was the best I've ever eaten and sometimes when the ears were young we'd even eat the cob.)

In the morning Tom and I were drawn to the kitchen by the smell of a pot of oatmeal simmering on the back burner. Grandma would be wearing a well used apron over her dress (I never saw her in pants or rarely in a robe). Her hair would be wound up in a bun ready for the day. She would also offer us eggs or pancakes. Following the clean up and coffee, she would withdraw to her desk in her room. We instinctively knew it was her quiet time where she would read from her Bible or work on correspondence. How did she ever keep up with all of us................11 surviving children, numerous grandchildren, and friends? I used to peek in her room every once in awhile to see her reflectively sitting at her desk overlooking her porch with planters full of geraniums, petunias, and other colorful flowers.

COFFEE That word deserves its own paragraph. The coffee was boiled on the back burner and I think I remember it sometimes had egg shells and maybe even a dash of salt in the container to help flavor the brew. This hot, strong, fully caffeinated beverage was served at breakfast, mid-morning, noon, afternoon, dinnertime, and again at 10:00 pm before bedtime, especially if there were additional adults in the house. Fresh sweet rolls or cookies purchased from the local bakery nearly always accompanied this occasion. We children didn't drink the coffee but we certainly enjoyed the sweet treats. How did Grandma sleep after drinking all that caffeine?

My family spent only one Christmas in Battle Lake when I was very young. I know I loved being there for that celebration but did not like most of the food that was served.............the smelly lutefisk is one I can't forget. On the other hand her deep fried rosettes, sprinkled with confectioner's sugar, were delicious.

I was always aware that when Grandma was nine years old she had emigrated from Norway with her family. When she married Adsit, she was not allowed to speak Norwegian in the house. He wanted only English spoken and as I remember she spoke English fluently and without an accent. I wonder how she felt having to disavow her culture? Other than "uff da" I don't remember her speaking any Norwegian to us.

I remember only a little physical affection from her, but I always knew I was loved unconditionally. She exuded warmth, humor, and joy in of each of us. When we departed each summer, I remember her standing on the front porch waving good bye as we drove away. I wonder how many family pictures were taken on that front porch as we gathered around our beloved grandmother? My brother Tom and I would visit with her for two weeks each summer and they were my favorite two weeks of the year. When we drove away each time, I would cry; it would be a long year until I would return.

Notes on the Hatch Family

The Hatch Family

Adsit Hatch 1855 – 1929
        m. 1890
Louise Sahol Hatch 1871 – 1968

Children

Susan Louise 1890 – 1990
m. C. J. (Rack) Wittbecker , Herman Strander
daughter: Patricia Louise Turner
grandchildren: Diane, Paul, Mark and Susan Turner

Agnes Camille 1892 – 1984
m. Howard Harman

Irene 1894 – 1894

Charles Adsit 1895 – 1974

Harriet Olivia (Hattie) 1897 – 1976
m. George Witthoft
daughter: Harriet Louise Skora
grandchildren: David, Michael, Daniel, Mathew
and Dianne Skora

Edith Josephine 1899 – 1991
m. Leonard Langen
children: Owen Thron Langen, Mary Louise Auren Weil
grandchildren: John and James Auren

Clara Olive 1901 – 1989
m. Elmer Hanson
daughter: Elizabeth Louise Spain
grandchildren: Linda, Sandra and Steven Spain

Alice Olea 1902 – 1995
m. Joseph Greenbaum

Irene Elizabeth (Bessie)   1904 – 1999
m. Robert Glennon
children: Jeanette Louise Hanson, Rosemary Louise Freitag,
Elizabeth Louise McIntire and Roberta Louise Toole
grandchildren: Roberta, Richard and Daniel Hanson
Patricia, Teresa, Virginia and William Freitag
Homer, Robert, Nancy, John and Elizabeth McIntire
Mary, Douglas, and William Timothy Toole

Dorothy Harriet   1906 – 2000
m. Robert Shepard
children: Sarah Ann Louise Shepard, Mary Louise Phillips
Stephen Henry Shepard and William Robert Shepard
grandchildren: Jane, John and Nicholas Veronis
Edward and Owen Phillips,
Robert, Ann, Stephen and Susan Shepard
Zachary and Peter Shepard

Hester Hildreth   1908 – 1994
m. H.G. Bissinger

Lorenzo Rexford (Ren / Rex) 1913 – 1973
m. Katharine Bell
children: Susan Katharine Devine, Thomas Wells Hatch,
Michael Allen Hatch, Katharine Louise Giteck
grandchildren: Kristin, Kelly and Katharine Devine
Jessica, Jethro, Joseph, Conner, Alice, and Greta Hatch
Katharine, Elizabeth and Anne Hatch
Kara Singleton and Ross Giteck

Elizabeth Hatch (Libby)   1884 – 1903 (Adsit's daughter)
m. Sander Nylander

Leila Isolde Nylander   1906 – 1934

Notes on the Hatch Family

Elizabeth Hatch (Libby) Nylander
Libby was the daughter of Adsit Hatch and Carrie Tweeten. After her mother died, Adsit married Louise Sahol. Libby grew up in the large Hatch family. She married Sander Nylander in the parlor at the Hatch house in 1903. Nine months later she died of Tuberculosis.

Susan Louise Wittbecker Strander
Sue went to the University of Minnesota and became a teacher. She married C.J. (Rack) Wittbecker. They lived in Fergus Falls with their daughter, Patricia. Sue was active in the D.A.R. and was a long time volunteer in the city. She loved animals, especially dogs, and was a great bridge player. After Rack died, Sue reconfigured her large house and opened a nursing home, which she ran for many years. Later she married Herman Strander, who had been Rack's best friend. In her last years, Sue lived with her granddaughter, Diane, and died in 1990 at age 100.

Agnes Camille Harman
Agnes graduated from the Conservatory of Music in Minneapolis where she studied piano. When she found she could not make a living in music she became a nurse, training at St. Mary's Hospital in Rochester, Minnesota. Later she became a hospital administrator, leading a major hospital in Chillicothe Ohio. She married Dr. Howard Harman in 1945 and was happy to have two step-sons, Gabe and Fred. Agnes was known for her wonderful good humor. She loved to travel and was very active in her community. She lived to be 92 and died in 1984.

Charles Adsit Hatch
Charlie graduated from Hamline University and then received a law degree from the University of Minnesota. He went on to have a distinguished career as a judge. He came home to Battle Lake often and maintained a huge garden there of both flowers and vegetables. He won blue ribbons for his irises and his corn was legendary. He loved dogs and at one time raised prize winning bulldogs. He was often a judge at dog shows. Charles was an avid fisherman and a hunter. With his Masonic lodge, he spent countless hours volunteering on behalf of the Shrine

Children's Hospital. He took care of his mother in the house they shared until she died. Charlie was a quintessential uncle and when he died at 78 in 1974, he left the house in a trust for his nephews and nieces.

Harriet Olivia Witthoft
Hattie went by the name of Harriet when she grew up. She studied nursing in Minneapolis and had a long, successful career, both in hospitals and as a private nurse. In 1928 she married George Witthoft, and they lived in Chicago. They had one daughter, Harriet Louise. Harriet was very active in the war effort during World War II. She was an excellent gardener and bridge player. For a time, she helped out her sister, Sue, at her nursing home in Minnesota. When Harriet retired from nursing, she lived in California, with her daughter, also a nurse, and her family including her four grandsons and one granddaughter. She died in 1976 at age 78.

Edith Josephine Langen
Edith married Leonard Langen in 1921 and they lived in Fergus Falls. They had two children, Owen and Mary Louise. The great sadness in Edith's life was losing Owen in World War II. Edith loved gardening, and she was very accomplished at needlepoint and other crafts. Those artistic skills were often used as part of her volunteer work. Her greatest interest was in writing; she wrote lovely poetry and essays and many stories about her family. Edith spent her last years in Arizona near her daughter, Mary, and was especially close to her two grandsons, John and Jim. She died in 1991 at age 92.

Clara Olive Hanson
Clara went to Minneapolis to study secretarial work. In 1922, she married Dr. Elmer Hanson. They lived in Park Rapids and had a daughter, Betty. After Elmer died, Clara became an accomplished secretary. She retired at 65 but went on to work part time for twenty more years. She lived in Omaha to be near her daughter and her family. She spent a great deal of time with her three grandchildren, and often amused them with wonderful stories that she made up. Later she wrote a children's book based on those tales. Clara was 88 when she died in 1989.

Alice Olea Greenbaum

Alice was a natural born teacher. She began her career in a one room school house but in a few years was at Columbia University getting a graduate degree. She was a master first-grade teacher in New York for thirty-five years. She often came home to Battle Lake during the summers where she pursued her interest in gardening and antiques and earned her role as a special aunt to all her nieces and nephews. She continued doing research at Columbia on early childhood education and she wrote many stories based on the Hatch family. Alice married fellow math teacher, Joseph Greenbaum, in 1954 and she was happy to have his daughter, Louise and her children as part of her family. She died in 1995 at age 93.

Irene Elizabeth Glennon

Irene was called Bessie and Bess for most of her life. She was sickly when she was young and the family was constantly worrying about her health. But along the way she began to thrive and lived a long and vigorous life. She taught school in South Dakota where she married Dr. Robert Glennon. They had four daughters, Jeanette, Rosemary, Betty and Bobby Lou. Bess was a long time president of the school board in the city of Miller and was an active volunteer in scouting and other civic affairs there. Family history was important to Bess and she wrote several books about her ancestors. She loved playing bridge and doing crochet. She made beautiful quilts for her daughters, her fifteen grandchildren and many great-grand children. Bess died at 94 in Fergus Falls in 1999.

Dorothy Harriet Shepard

Dorothy went to St. Paul to secretarial school with her cousin, Leila. After working for a few years she married Robert Shepard. They lived in Duluth and raised four children, Sarah, Mary, Steve, and Bill. Dorothy was artistic and athletic. She loved the outdoors and was playing golf and swimming well into her later years. She was a long-time hospital volunteer, and a dedicated gardener with a passion for roses and lilacs. As an avid bridge player, she often said she was lucky in cards and lucky in love. Loved by her four children, eleven grand children and many great-grandchildren, she died in California, in 2000 at age 94.

Hester Hildreth Bissinger

After high school, Hester went to Chicago to live with her sister Harriet, who helped her with her education. She studied dance and theater and became a photographic model. She married H.G. Bissinger in 1932 and they settled in New Jersey. After retirement, they came back to live in Minnesota, on a lake near Battle Lake. Hester always had a beautiful garden. In her later years, Hester lived in Fergus Falls and was very close to her sister, Irene. She died at 84 in 1994.

Lorenzo Rexford Hatch

Lorenzo was named after his grandfather and called Ren or Rennie, and later in life, Rex. The youngest of the large family, he was much loved by all, especially his mother. Ren went to the University of Minnesota in Minneapolis. He married Katharine Bell and they had four children, Susan, Tom, Mike and Katharine. Ren had an active business career in Iowa, Wisconsin and Minnesota. He was a great cook and enjoyed fishing and hunting and loved dogs. After Katharine died, he retired to the Hatch house where he lived with his brother, Charlie. He made many good friends in Battle Lake, before he died of a heart ailment at the early age of 60 in 1973.

Leila Isolde Nylander was born in 1906 and was Louise's niece. Leila came to live with the Hatch family in 1908, when she was two years old, after her mother, Helga, died of tuberculosis. Helga was Louise's younger sister. Leila's father, Sander Nylander, died of T.B. in 1908. She was raised in the family as one of their own and called Louise "Mama", as the other children did. After high school, she went to St. Paul with her cousin, Dorothy, where they attended secretarial school. After graduation Leila got a job in an office and was engaged to be married. About this time, she began to spell her name, Leela and to sign her name, Lee. In 1932 when she was 25 she became ill with tuberculosis and was admitted to a sanatorium in Walker Minnesota. Her fiancé visited her every week until she died there in 1934 at age 28. Leila's disease may have been a re-infection of a lesion formed on her lung as a child. At that time T.B. was almost always fatal; the only treatment was rest and nursing care. (Ten years after Leila died, Streptomycin was discovered as a cure for the disease.) Leila and Louise had a special loving relationship and wrote to each other often while she was at the sanatorium.

Sunday

Mother Darling,

Today is "Mother's Day" – and how I wish I could have been with you, darling – have thought of you all day long – and have been so thankful that I have you – Mama Sweetheart. No one could be more wonderful and sweet to me. – Have been listening to such beautiful Mother's songs and programs all day – they made me so lonesome for you – a long time again – feel much stronger now too – Mama Dear – Your prayers have done such wonders for me –

It makes me so mad when I cry when you come up – but it's just cause I'm so tickled to see you – and wish I could get up all well and be with you always – really. Mama – I don't worry a speck – and course I'm going to get well – have all the Faith in the world that I am – My stomach isn't T.B. I'm sure – and when that's o.k. I'm sure I can fight any thing else with your prayers Mama Dear – and God's wonderful blessings –

Nite, Mama Darling. I love you just millions, will write Sue a note and you again soon – Am really most fine again – so don't worry.

All my love, Lee

P.S. The lily is still so pretty – every one just raves about it –

Charles and Louise

2/11/38

*If I were to use
a thousand words.
They could not tell you
more than this.
I love you,
Dear Valentine.*

Dearest Mother: Years ago when I was a very little boy, this is what I'd have sent you. And after all, I'm still that little boy, somewhat grown up.
Love Son Chas

From the Diary of Charles Hatch
1913

Dec. 24:

Went skating in morning. Was going out in ice boat with Clarence Olson, but I had to give it up as I got too cold.

We had a very fine Xmas evening. Our tree was a very beautiful one, and we trimmed it as nicely as possible. It was placed in the usual place in the middle of the west wall of the parlor, in front of mother's old mill painting. S.A. Nylander and Murray Bates were the only outsiders with us. About seven thirty we all assembled in the parlor about the tree. We had a short program; each of the little girls gave the pieces they had prepared for the Xmas trees at the different churches. Sue, Ag, and Edith and I sang "Those Evening Bells", an old favorite of Dad's. Then Dad read the Xmas story from the Bible. This was the first time he had ever done this, and it surely was very nice. Then before giving out the presents, Sue and I sang Home Sweet Home. I got a bathrobe from Sue and Ag, and Mother; a box of stationary from Sue and Ag. A box of candy from Irene J., a book from Martha; a black and orange jersey from Loken and Berg, some handkerchiefs from the children. I gave dad cigars (box), a set of combs to Mother, a locket and chain for both Sue and Ag, bracelets for the rest of the girls.

Friday

Dearest Mother,

Just a note to let you know we are all fine and especially to let you know that I will be thinking of you on Mother's Day.

As you have been told many times Mother, no family was ever blessed with a more beautiful, more understanding or more wonderful Mother and I know that I, as well as the others appreciate those facts more & more as I get older.

Other children may have had more material things but no child ever had a finer Mother. And what is more important than that?

I have been working hard both at the office & at home in the yard. I have put in radishes and onions & plan to have a few tomato plants. Also have transplanted flowers, planted trees, etc.

The big blackout is coming on soon tonight & I want to get this mailed before it does come on. As it is nearly nine, I must hurry.

Am very anxious to get home again. Probably won't be able to get there often or long this summer but will spend all possible time there that can be arranged.

Good Night & God Bless You.

   Love,

    Son Ren

A letter to Louise from Ren, who lived in Minneapolis with his family. This was written during W.W. II when cities and towns across the country were required to turn off all lights at night in case of a bomb attack.

Holiday Greetings
            Christmas 1954

Dear Mother —

    Through the years —
    Thank you for your love.
    Thank you for your understanding
    Thank you — For being you —

            My Love —
            Your Own
            Ron.

Agnes Camille, Harriet and Edith were all born on Oct. 21st, a few years apart and all had red hair. Bessie was born later on Oct. 23rd. Their birthday tradition was to have a very large cake for the older girls and a cupcake on top for Bessie. Later, Edith's daughter, Mary, submitted the story and it was published in "Ripley's Believe or Not", a newspaper feature that told about unusual events.

A note about hair:
As mentioned, Agnes, Harriet and Edith all had their father's red hair, as did Charles and Dorothy. Sue, Alice and Clara had their mother's luxurious dark hair and Bess, Hester and Ren were fair-haired blondes.

Tuberculosis was epidemic in the early 1900's and while none of the Hatch children were infected, many relatives were.
Here are some of those who died of the disease.
Carrie Hatch – died 1884 – Adsit's first wife and the mother of
Elizabeth (Libby) Hatch Nylander – died 1903 – Adsit's daughter.
Helga Sahol Hatch – died 1908 – Louise's sister.
Albert Hanson – Helga's first husband – died 1902
   also Olive and Hazel Hanson, Albert and Helga's daughters.
Sander Nylander – died 1916 – married first to Libby Hatch and then to Helga. Many in his family also died of T.B.
Leila Nylander – died 1934 – daughter of Helga and Sander - niece of Louise
Lorenzo Hatch Jr. – died 1906 – brother of Adsit in Wisconsin.

The Hatch House

The Hatch House   1920 & 2000

One of the games we used to play was "Fire in the Opera House." We would all stand at the top of the stairway and listen to one of Charlie's opera records. Then someone would yell, "Fire in the Opera House!" and we would all tumble down the stairs. We played that for years until someone was hurt and then Mama put a stop to it.

From the Journal of Dorothy Hatch Shepard

Hoyt Music sold a Cable piano to A.C. Hatch, Saturday
From *The Battle Lake Review Oct. 19th, 1906*

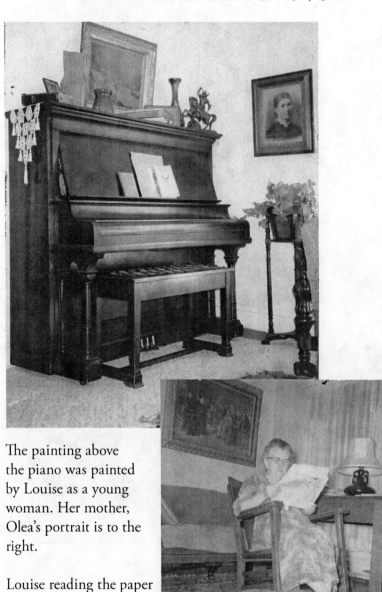

The painting above the piano was painted by Louise as a young woman. Her mother, Olea's portrait is to the right.

Louise reading the paper with Rocky at her feet.

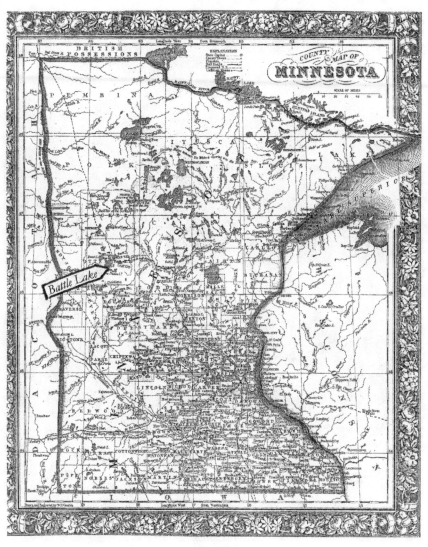

1862 Map

Thanks to all the Hatch cousins who helped with suggestions for this book, and for their support and love for the old house: Mary W., Rosemary, Betty M., Harriet, Sarah, Steve, Bill, Tom, Mike, and Kathy.

In remembrance:
Owen, Bobby Lou, Patty, Jeanette and Betty S.

Thanks to Edward for his editorial assistance.

Mary and Susan

Lovingly Mother.

Breinigsville, PA USA
21 July 2010

242218BV00003B/1/P